1000 Ninja Foodi Pressure Cooker Complete Cookbook

Amazing & Easy Air Fry, Pressure Cook, Slow Cook, Dehydrate, and More Recipes for Beginners and Advanced Users

Edna Negrin

© Copyright 2020 - All rights reserved.

The content contained within this book may not be reproduced, duplicated or transmitted without direct written permission from the author or the publisher.

Under no circumstances will any blame or legal responsibility be held against the publisher, or author, for any damages, reparation, or monetary loss due to the information contained within this book. Either directly or indirectly.

Legal Notice:

This book is copyright protected. This book is only for personal use. You cannot amend, distribute, sell, use, quote or paraphrase any part, or the content within this book, without the consent of the author or publisher.

Disclaimer Notice:

Please note the information contained within this document is for educational and entertainment purposes only. All effort has been executed to present accurate, up to date, and reliable, complete information. No warranties of any kind are declared or implied. Readers acknowledge that the author is not engaging in the rendering of legal, financial, medical or professional advice. The content within this book has been derived from various sources. Please consult a licensed professional before attempting any techniques outlined in this book.

By reading this document, the reader agrees that under no circumstances is the author responsible for any losses, direct or indirect, which are incurred as a result of the use of information contained within this document, including, but not limited to, — errors, omissions, or inaccuracies.

Table of Contents

Introduction 7

What is the Ninja Foodi Pressure Cooker? 7

The functions of Ninja Foodi Pressure Cooker 7

Tips for Using the Ninja Foodi Pressure Cooker 8

Chapter 1: Breakfast Recipes 10

Chia Slow Cook 10

Marinated Eggs 10

Breakfast Panini 10

Tortilla Ham Wraps 11

Veggie Frittata 11

Stuffed Peppers with Eggs 11

Light Chicken Casserole 12

Egg Muffins 12

Creamy Cauliflower Rice 13

Tomato Cups 13

Hot Pepper Eggs 13

Cheesy Chorizo Topping 14

Cauliflower Rice with Bacon 14

Ham Frittata 14

Breakfast Yogurt 15

Breakfast Strata 15

Egg Balls 15

Broccoli Rice 16

Spinach Muffins 16

Sweet Egg Toasts 16

Seeds Mix 17

Zucchini Pasta with Chicken 17

Breakfast Pasta Casserole 17

Egg Sandwiches 18

Chicken Quiche 18

Zucchini Scramble 19

Chocolate Slow Cook 19

Cauliflower Rice Balls 19

Coconut Porridge with Cream 20

Cottage Cheese Soufflé 20

Creamy Porridge 20

Cauliflower Balls 21

Cinnamon Chia Pudding 21

Creamy Pumpkin Puree 21

Bread Pudding 22

Creamy Mac Cups 22

Scotch Eggs 22

Flax Meal with Almonds 23

Chapter 2: Snacks and Appetizers Recipes ... 24

Zucchini Tots 24

Shallot Pancakes 24

Zucchini Muffins with Poppy Seeds 25

Deviled Eggs 25

Herbed Butter 25

Broccoli Tots 26

Glazed Walnuts 26

Wrapped Halloumi Cheese 26

Onion Rings 26

Cheesy Bombs 27

Garlic Tomato Slices 27

Creamy Shallots with Mushrooms 28

Meatloaf 28

Glazed Jalapeno Slices 28

Cauliflower Fritters 29

Breadsticks 29

Veggie Nuggets 29

Chicken Nuggets 30

Carrot Spirals 30

Stuffed Dates 31

Dried Tomatoes 31

Crunchy Chicken Skin 31

Gratin Mustard Potatoes 32

Cashew Cream 32

Chapter 3: Chicken and Poultry Recipes 33

Roasted Crisp Whole Chicken 33

Glazed Chicken Drumsticks 33

Green Curry Chicken Thai Style 34

Herbed Cornish Hen 34

Duck with Berries Mix 35

Garlic Duck and Apples 35

Traditional Chicken 'n Dumplings 36

Lemony Whole Chicken 36

Turkey Potato Pie 37

Garlic Chicken in Creamy Tuscan Style 37

Bacon-Wrapped Chicken Breasts 38

Spinach Stuffed Chicken Breasts 38

Tasty Sesame-Honeyed Chicken 39

Thyme Duck 40

Hot Turkey Cutlets 40

Duck with Asparagus 40

Savory 'n Aromatic Chicken Adobo 41

Parsley Duck and Fennel 41

Ginger-Balsamic Glazed Chicken 41

Chapter 4: Beef, Pork and Lamb Recipes 43

Mustard Dredged Pork Chops 43

Crazy Greek Lamb Gyros 43

Healthy Cranberry Keto-Friendly BBQ Pork 43

Mesmerizing Beef Sirloin Steak 44

Epic Beef Sausage Soup 44

Mesmerizing Pork Carnitas 45

Authentic Beginner Friendly Pork Belly 45

The Indian Beef Delight 45

Warm and Beefy Meat Loaf 46

The Ultimate One-Pot Beef Roast 46

Deliciously Spicy Pork Salad Bowl 47

Decisive Kalua Pork 47

Perfect Sichuan Pork Soup 48

Special "Swiss" Pork chops 48

Fresh Korean Braised Ribs 49

Wise Corned Beef 49

Easy-Going Kid Friendly Pork Chops 49

The Classical Corned Beef and Cabbage 50

Elegant Beef Curry 50

Chapter 5: Fish and Seafood Recipes 52

Mackerel and Zucchini Patties 52

Shrimp and Tomato Delight 52

Fish Pie 52

Paprika Salmon 53

Cool Shrimp Zoodles 53

Calamari in Tomato Sauce 53

Stuffed Snapper with Onions 54

Cod Chowder 54

Awesome Sock-Eye Salmon 55

Mackerel Salad 55

Tasty Cuttlefish 56

Spicy Whitebait 56

Monkfish Stew 57

Seafood Paella 57

Fish Curry 58

Red Chili Anchovy 58

Parsley Marinated Shrimps 58

Halibut with the Soy Ginger Sauce 59

Cod Stew 59

Sriracha Shrimp 60

Tuna and Shirataki Noodles Salad 60

Tomato Snapper 61

Marjoram Salmon 61

Crunchy Cod 61

Smoked Salmon Bars 62

Sweet Mackerel 62

Fish Tacos 63

Mussel Soup 63

Chapter 6: Vegetables Recipes 64

Lime Cabbage and Bacon 64

Potatoes and Lemon Sauce 64

Soy Kale 64

Chili Eggplant and Kale 65

Minty Radishes 65

Parsley Kale and Leeks 65

Carrots and Walnuts Salad 66

Pine Nuts Okra and Leeks 66

Sesame Radish and Leeks 66

Lime Broccoli and Cauliflower 67

Napa Cabbage and Carrots 67

Zucchinis and Spinach Mix 67

Creamy Kale 68

Radish and Apples Mix 68

Pomegranate Radish Mix 68

Garlic Red Bell Peppers Mix 69

Chives Beets and Carrots 69

Balsamic Cabbage and Endives 69

Lemony Leeks and Carrots 70

Kale and Parmesan 70

Chapter 7: Side Dishes Recipes 71

    Zucchini Noodles 71

    Wrapped Asparagus 71

    Cabbage Hash Brown 71

    Red Beetroot Salad 72

    Mashed Turnips with Chives 72

    Butternut Squash with Garlic 72

    Sweet Glazed Onion 73

    Cabbage Rice 73

    Sautéed Spinach 73

    Carrot Puree 74

    Keto Tortillas 74

    Creamed Onions Halves 74

    Green Asian-style Zucchini Strips 75

    Japanese Style Black Bean Pasta 75

    Cream Spinach 75

    Balsamic Onions 76

    Turmeric Mushroom Hats 76

    Spaghetti Squash 76

    Shumai 77

    Garlic Cauliflower Florets 77

    Tender Collard Greens 77

    Celery Root Cubes 78

    Cauliflower Rice 78

    Broccoli Salad 79

Chapter 8: Desserts Recipes 80

    Chocolate Topping 80

    Blueberry Muffins 80

    Vanilla Ice Cream 80

    Chocolate Bacon 80

    Savory Baked Apples 81

    Chocolate Muffins 81

    Pineapple Whisked Cake 81

    Lime Pie 82

    Sweet Pudding 82

    Strawberry Cheesecake 82

    Pumpkin Pudding 83

    Cinnamon Apple Cake 83

    Hot Vanilla Shake 84

    Strawberry Pie 84

    Blondies 84

    Pumpkin Cake 85

    Lemon Curd 85

    Applesauce 85

    Keto Donuts 86

    Chocolate Lava Ramekins 86

    Grated Pie 86

    Lemon Flan 87

Introduction

What is the Ninja Foodi Pressure Cooker?

Well, Ninja Foodi is possibly the latest and one of the most versatile and revolutionary multi-cooker to date that every chef and budding enthusiast should have! At its heart, the Ninja Foodi is an electric pressure cooker, but behind its seemingly innocent façade, it's much more than that.

The Ninja Foodi Pressure Cooker can speed up your meal making, slow cook to multi-task, sear, and sauté ingredients to build flavor, and create endless recipes with our versatile pressure cookers.

Sauté veggies; cook grains and rice; slow cook stews and chilis; sear and braise meats; and sous vide seafood—all in one pot.

When it comes to pressure cooking, we want to make your kitchen experience as easy, convenient, and as delicious as possible.

This basically means that using the Ninja Foodi, you will be able to make your favorite Keto-Friendly dish ranging from stews, meat, snacks, and even desserts!

Using the dehydrator feature, the Ninja Foodi will also allow you to preserve and fruits and vegetables.

And the best part? Despite having a myriad of amazing features, the Ninja is still a very accessible and user-friendly device that anyone can use!

The functions of Ninja Foodi Pressure Cooker

The pre-set cooking buttons allow you to cook foods without the guesswork thus you can cook even the most complicated food even if you are a novice. With the preset cooking button, the Ninja Foodi will be the one to cook the food based on the setting you have chosen using pre-programmed temperature and circulation so that you can cook food depending on the setting that you have chosen. When cooking food using the Ninja Foodi, it is important that you become familiar with the pre-set cooking buttons work.

Pressure: this allows you to cook food through pressure cooking. With this pre-set cooking button, it allows you to cook food 70% faster compared to conventional methods.

Sear/sauté: turn your Ninja Foodi into a sear buttoning pan with this function. It is good in sear buttoning meat, sautéing, or toasting spices. Do not use any lid with this pre-set button. You can also use it to simmer or thicken sauces. You can use the lid for simmering but make sure that it is not sealed in place. This pre-set cooking button does not come with a time adjustment so just press the Start/Stop button if you want to start or stop this function.

Air crisp: this allows you to transform the multicooker into a Ninja Foodi. This setting cooks the food between 3000f and 4000f. Make sure to preheat the ninja food first for at least five minutes before adding the ingredients. Use the crisping lid for this pre-set cooking button.

Slow cook: this pre-set cooking button allows you to cook food at low temperature similar with a slow cooker. Use the pressure lid but do not set the vent to sealed. You can adjust the cooking time between 4 and 12 hours depending on the type of food that you are cooking. The keep warm function will turn on once the cooking time is complete.

Steam: steam your food gently at high temperature. Use at least one cup of liquid to steam your food and use the accompanying rack. Use the pressure lid and set the vent to seal for this function.

Broil: this pre-set cooking button allows you to caramelize or sear button the surface of your food. Use the crisping lid with this function. There is no temperature adjustment for this pre-set cooking button, but you can adjust the cooking time depending on what you are cooking. And just like the air crisper, preheat the unit first before adding the ingredients.

Dehydrate: this pre-set cooking button allows you to dehydrate different kinds of ingredients so that you can make healthy snacks. Dehydrate foods from 105°F to 195°F. We recommend that you get the dehydrating rack, so you have more area to dehydrate your food.

Bake/roast: this setting converts the multicooker into an oven. This allows you to cook food between 2000F and 4000F.use the crisping lid to roast meats, veggies, or make baked goodies. Make sure to preheat the unit first before putting in the food.

Tips for Using the Ninja Foodi Pressure Cooker

With 14 multiple layers of safety, Ninja Foodi allows cooking to cook without worrying about their safety in any manner. But you can further boost your confidence by following a few tips before beginning your cooking experience with Ninja Foodi.

Here are all those tips you should use when using Ninja Foodi as a newbie:

Go through the manual instructions

This pot comes with simple and understandable manual instructions. So, that should not be a problem. Just make sure you don't jump right into using the pot without reading the manual. Give a few minutes before you are ready to cook your very first meal.

Understand every function

Ninja Foodi is a multicooker, which comes with various cooking functionalities. You have already read about the functions of pressure cooking, air frying, steaming, searing, sautéing, baking, crisping, and others. Other functions include Tender Crisp, steaming, and others.

To effectively utilize this appliance, it would be wise to understand every function and its benefit before moving forward. Using this knowledge of functionality, you can choose your dishes wisely and cook more efficiently.

Pick simple dishes in the beginning

The diversity of cooking styles in Ninja Foodi can seem overwhelming to newbies. So, it is better to relax and cook simple dishes initially.

You can start with simple one-pot stews and soups to make yourself comfortable with the control panel and functions of the pot.

Eventually, you will find yourself remembering the process and utilizing each and every function of the pot. Then, you can move toward more complex food options and cook multi-combination meals in one go.

Practice as frequently as possible

Cooking once or twice a week won't help if you are a newbie at pressure cooking. You need to frequently cook dishes as many times as possible. The more you cook the better you will get at using all the functions.

Ninja Foodi saves from wasting time in thawing a frozen food. So, you can simply transfer a food straight from the refrigerator to the pot. The air fryer technology works with pressure cooking to make your food tender and crispy. Plus, your food keeps the juices intact.

By this way, you can cook more in lesser time and enjoy delicious chicken, pork, beef, and other food items. But it all comes down to how many times you cook initially to make yourself more and more competent with the functions of the pot.

Utilize attached accessories

Along with a nonstick cooking pot, Ninja Foodi comes with other attached accessories such as a crisping lid, a basket, a reversible rack, and a pressure lid as well. Every accessory Servings: a purpose. From sealing the pot to frying it internally, every cooking advantage is possible only when you use all the attached accessories efficiently.

Try a new dish every day

To improve your cooking capabilities, you need to go beyond your comfort zone every day. Of course, you start with simple dishes in the beginning, but don't get stuck in those same dishes. Cooking is fun when you try new dishes every day. And thanks to Ninja Foodi, you will have all the functions available in one pot to cook different desserts, vegetables, poultry, fish, and red meat recipes.

Chapter 1: Breakfast Recipes

Chia Slow Cook

Prep time: 5 minutes| Cook time: **5 minutes**| Servings: 4

Ingredients:

- 1 cup Greek yogurt
- 1 cup of water
- 1 cup chia seeds
- 1 tablespoon liquid stevia
- ½ teaspoon cinnamon
- 1 teaspoon lemon zest
- 2 apples
- ¼ teaspoon salt
- 1 teaspoon clove

Directions:

Combine the water and Greek yogurt together and blend well. Transfer the liquid mixture in the pressure cooker and add chia seeds. Stir the mixture and sprinkle it with the liquid stevia, cinnamon, lemon zest, salt, and cloves. Peel the apples and chop them into small chunks. Add the chopped apple in the pressure cooker and stir well. Close the lid, and set the pressure cooker mode to "Steam." Cook for 7 minutes. When the dish is cooked, remove it from the pressure cooker and mix well gently. Serve the chia Slow Cook hot. Enjoy.

Nutrition: calories 259, fat 13.3, fiber 12.8, carbs 29.5, protein 8.5

Marinated Eggs

Prep time: 10 minutes| Cook time: **5 minutes**| Servings: **5**

Ingredients:

- 1 teaspoon red chili flakes
- ½ cup of water
- 5 eggs, boiled
- 1 teaspoon salt
- ⅓ cup of soy sauce
- 1 teaspoon cilantro
- ½ teaspoon ground black pepper
- 1 tablespoon lemon juice
- 1 tablespoon sugar
- 2 tablespoons mirin

Directions:

Peel the eggs, and transfer them to the pressure cooker. Combine the water, chili flakes, salt, soy sauce, cilantro, ground black pepper, lemon juice, and mirin in a mixing bowl. Stir the mixture well until smooth, then pour the mixture in the pressure cooker. Stir it gently, close the lid, and set the pressure cooker mode to "Sauté". Cook for 5 minutes. Transfer the mixture to casserole dish and let it cool. When the eggs are cool, serve them right away and store in the refrigerator to serve later.

Nutrition: calories 189, fat 12.8, fiber 1, carbs 7.7, protein 10

Breakfast Panini

Prep time: 5 minutes| **Cook time:** 2 minutes| Servings: 4

Ingredients:

- 1 banana
- 8 slices low carb bread
- 2 tablespoons butter
- 1 teaspoon vanilla extract
- 1 teaspoon cinnamon

Directions:

Peel the banana and slice it. Spread bread with the butter from both sides. Sprinkle the bread slices with the vanilla. Add banana and make sandwiches. Transfer the sandwiches in the pressure cooker and close the lid. Set the mode to "Sauté," and cook for 1 minute on each side. Remove the sandwiches from the pressure cooker and rest briefly before serving.

Nutrition: calories 127, fat 6.4, fiber 3.1, carbs 14.3, protein 4.4

Tortilla Ham Wraps

Prep time: 10 minutes| **Cook time:** 10 minutes| **Servings:** 5

Ingredients:

- 5 almond flour tortillas
- 10 ounces ham
- 2 tomatoes
- 1 cucumber
- 1 red onion
- 1 tablespoon mayonnaise
- 2 tablespoons olive oil
- 2 tablespoons ketchup
- 1 teaspoon basil
- 1 teaspoon paprika
- ½ teaspoon cayenne pepper
- 4 ounces lettuce

Directions:

Slice the tomatoes and chop the cucumbers. Chop the ham. Peel the red onion and chop it. Combine the mayonnaise, olive oil, ketchup, basil, paprika, and cayenne pepper and stir the mixture. Spread the tortillas with the mayonnaise mixture and add chopped ham. Sprinkle the dish with the chopped onion, sliced tomatoes, and chopped cucumbers. Add lettuce and wrap the tortillas. Transfer the tortilla wraps in the pressure cooker and close the lid. Set the pressure cooker mode at "Steam," and cook for 10 minutes. Remove the dish from the pressure cooker and rest briefly.

Nutrition: calories 249, fat 15, fiber 4.1, carbs 14.7, protein 15.6

Veggie Frittata

Prep time: 10 minutes| **Cook time:** 15 minutes| **Servings:** 6

Ingredients:

- 10 eggs
- 1 cup of coconut milk
- 1 teaspoon salt
- ½ teaspoon ground black pepper
- 1 sweet bell pepper
- ½ jalapeno pepper
- 3 tomatoes
- 1 zucchini
- 1 tablespoon butter
- 5 ounces asparagus
- ½ cup cilantro

Directions:

Beat the eggs in the mixing bowl until combined. Add the coconut milk and butter and combine. Sprinkle the mixture with the salt and, ground black pepper and mix well. Chop the zucchini, tomatoes, asparagus, and cilantro. Remove the seeds from the bell pepper and chop it. Slice the jalapeno pepper. Transfer the egg mixture to the pressure cooker. Top with the vegetables and cilantro. Close the lid, and set the pressure cooker mode to "Steam." Cook for 15 minutes. Remove the frittata from the pressure cooker. Serve immediately.

Nutrition: calories 145, fat 11.4, fiber 1.7, carbs 5.4, protein 7.1

Stuffed Peppers with Eggs

Prep time: 10 minutes| **Cook time:** 15 minutes| **Servings:** 3

Ingredients:

- 4 eggs, boiled
- 9 ounces feta cheese
- 1 tablespoon butter
- 2 sweet bell peppers
- 1 teaspoon salt
- 1 cup chicken stock
- ½ cup cilantro
- 1 teaspoon heavy cream

- 2 tablespoons sour cream
- 1 tablespoon tomato paste

Directions:

Remove the seeds from the bell peppers. Peel the eggs, and stuff the bell peppers with the eggs. Chop the feta cheese and cilantro and combine them together. Sprinkle the cheese mixture with the salt, cream, sour cream, and tomato paste. Blend the mixture together until smooth. Add the cream mixture to the bell peppers. Add the butter in the pressure cooker, and transfer the stuffed peppers to the pot. Add chicken stock and close the lid. Set the pressure cooker mode to "Steam," and cook for 15 minutes. When the cooking time ends, let the dish rest briefly.

Nutrition: calories 513, fat 37.2, fiber 1, carbs 17.23, protein 28

Light Chicken Casserole

Prep time: 15 minutes| **Cook time:** 30 minutes| **Servings:** 6

Ingredients:

- 1 pound chicken breast fillets
- 4 egg yolks
- 1 onion
- 1 cup cream
- 10 ounces cheddar cheese
- 1 tablespoon butter
- ½ teaspoon ground black pepper
- 1 teaspoon salt
- 1 tablespoon lemon juice

Directions:

Cut the chicken into the strips, sprinkle it with the salt, lemon juice, and ground black pepper, and mix well. Grate the cheddar cheese. Peel and dice the onion. Combine the chopped onion with the butter and blend well. Transfer the chopped onion mixture in the pressure cooker. Make a layer from the chicken mixture. Whisk the egg yolks, and pour the mixture in the pressure cooker. Add cream and grated cheese. Close the lid, and set the pressure cooker mode to "Pressure." Cook for 30 minutes. When the casserole is cooked, let it cool briefly. Transfer the dish to the serving plate and serve.

Nutrition: calories 424, fat 27.7, fiber 2, carbs 26.58, protein 18

Egg Muffins

Prep time: 10 minutes| **Cook time:** 10 minutes| **Servings:** 6

Ingredients:

- 4 eggs
- ¼ cup almond flour
- 1 teaspoon salt
- ¼ cup cream
- 1 teaspoon baking soda
- 1 tablespoon lemon juice
- 1 white onion
- 5 ounces sliced bacon, cooked

Directions:

Beat the eggs using a whisk. Add almond flour and cream and whisk until smooth. Peel the onion and dice it. Chop the cooked bacon. Add the diced onion and chopped bacon in the egg mixture. Stir it carefully. Add salt, lemon juice, and baking soda and stir the mixture. Take muffin cups, and fill each one halfway with the egg dough. Transfer the muffin cups in the pressure cooker basket and close the lid. Set the pressure cooker mode to "Pressure," and cook the muffins for 10 minutes. When the muffins are cooked, remove them from the pressure cooker and rest briefly before serving.

Nutrition: calories 211, fat 15.7, fiber 0.9, carbs 3.6, protein 13.7

Creamy Cauliflower Rice

Prep time: 10 minutes| **Cook time:** 30 minutes| Servings: **3**

Ingredients:

- 1 cup cauliflower rice
- 1 cup heavy cream
- 1 cup of coconut milk
- ¼ cup of water
- 1 teaspoon salt
- 4 tablespoons Erythritol
- 1 teaspoon cinnamon

Directions:

Pour cream, coconut milk, and water in the pressure cooker. Stir the mixture gently and add salt, Erythritol, and cinnamon. Blend the mixture gently until you mixed well. Add cauliflower rice. Close the pressure cooker lid, and set the mode to "Slow Cook." Cook for 30 minutes. When the cooking time ends, open the lid and stir the mixture gently. Transfer the cooked dish to serving bowls and serve hot.

Nutrition: calories 343, fat 34.5, fiber 2.2, carbs 8.4, protein 4

Tomato Cups

Prep time: 5 minutes| **Cook time:** 3 minutes| Servings: 4

Ingredients:

- 4 big tomatoes
- 4 eggs
- 7 ounces ham
- 1 tablespoon chives
- 1 teaspoon mayonnaise
- ½ teaspoon butter
- 4 ounces Parmesan cheese
- ½ teaspoon salt

Directions:

Wash the tomatoes and remove the flesh, jelly, and seeds from them and add to a mixing bowl. Chop the ham and chives. Combine the chopped ham, chives, and tomato pieces together in a mixing bowl. Add mayonnaise, butter, and salt to the ham mixture and blend well. Grate the Parmesan cheese and beat the eggs in the empty tomato cups. Fill the cups with the ham mixture. Sprinkle them with the grated cheese. Wrap the tomato cups in aluminum foil and transfer them in the pressure cooker. Close the lid, and set the pressure cooker mode to "Sauté." Cook for 10 minutes. When the cooking time ends, remove the tomatoes from the pressure cooker and allow them to rest. Discard the foil and serve immediately.

Nutrition: calories 335, fat 19.8, fiber 1, carbs 12.17, protein 27

Hot Pepper Eggs

Prep time: 8 minutes| **Cook time:** 7 minutes| **Servings:** 3

Ingredients:

- 4 eggs
- 1 teaspoon cayenne pepper
- ½ teaspoon red chili flakes
- ½ teaspoon cilantro
- ½ teaspoon white pepper
- 1 avocado, pitted
- ½ cup sour cream
- 2 tablespoons butter
- 3 tablespoons chives

Directions:

Combine the cayenne pepper, chili flakes, cilantro, and white pepper together. Mix up the mixture. Chop the chives and slice the avocado. Combine the sour cream and butter together. Blend the mixture until smooth. Transfer the sour cream mixture in the pressure cooker. Add spice mixture. Beat the eggs in the pressure cooker. Add chives and avocado and close the lid. Set the pressure cooker mode to "Steam," and cook for 7 minutes. When the dish is cooked, remove it from the pressure cooker and serve it.

Nutrition: calories 410, fat 2, fiber 34.6, carbs 11.82, protein 15

Cheesy Chorizo Topping

Prep time: 10 minutes| **Cook time:** 8 minutes| **Servings:** 6

Ingredients:

- 8 ounces chorizo
- ⅓ cup tomato juice
- 1 teaspoon cilantro
- 1 tablespoon coconut flour
- 1 teaspoon olive oil
- 1 teaspoon butter
- 1 sweet bell peppers
- 3 eggs
- ⅓ cup of coconut milk
- 1 teaspoon coriander
- ¼ teaspoon thyme
- ⅓ cup fresh basil

Directions:

Combine the tomato juice, cilantro, coconut flour, olive oil, coriander, and thyme. Stir the mixture well. Remove the seeds from the bell peppers and chop it. Wash the fresh basil and chop it. Add coconut milk in the tomato juice mixture and beat the eggs. Blend the mixture using a hand mixer until smooth. Add the chopped peppers and butter. Chop the chorizo and add to the mixture. Transfer the mixture to the pressure cooker and close the lid. Set the pressure cooker mode to "Steam," and cook for 6 minutes. Open the lid and blend well carefully using a wooden spoon. Close the pressure cooker lid, and cook for 2 minutes. When the cooking time ends, let the dish rest briefly. Serve it immediately.

Nutrition: calories 260, fat 21.4, fiber 1.1, carbs 4.6, protein 12.7

Cauliflower Rice with Bacon

Prep time: 10 minutes| **Cook time:** 40 minutes| **Servings:** 7

Ingredients:

- 7 ounces sliced bacon
- 2 cups cauliflower rice
- 1 tablespoon olive oil
- 1 onion
- 4 cups chicken stock
- 1 teaspoon butter
- 1 teaspoon basil
- 1 teaspoon oregano
- 1 teaspoon thyme

Directions:

Chop the bacon and transfer it to the pressure cooker. Close the lid, and set the pressure cooker mode to «Sauté," and cook the bacon for 4 minutes. Open the lid and add the cauliflower rice. Sprinkle the mixture with the olive oil and stir. Add chicken stock, butter, basil, oregano, and thyme. Peel the onion and chop it. Sprinkle the cauliflower rice with the chopped onion, mix well, and close the lid. Set the pressure cooker mode to "Slow Cook," and cook for 40 minutes. When the dish is cooked, remove the cauliflower rice from the pressure cooker and stir. Transfer the dish to serving plates and serve.

Nutrition: calories 273, fat 19.6, fiber 8, carbs 25.03, protein 11

Ham Frittata

Prep time: 10 minutes| **Cook time:** 10 minutes| **Servings: 6**

Ingredients:

- 7 eggs
- ½ cup of coconut milk
- 1 teaspoon salt
- ½ teaspoon paprika
- ½ cup parsley

- 8 ounces ham
- 1 teaspoon white pepper
- 1 tablespoon lemon zest
- 1 teaspoon olive oil
- 1 tomato

Directions:

Beat the eggs in the mixing bowl. Add coconut milk, salt, paprika, white pepper, and lemon zest. Blend the mixture well using a hand mixer. Chop the tomato and add it to the egg mixture. Chop the ham, and top the egg mixture with the ham. Stir it carefully until smooth. Chop the parsley. Spray the pressure cooker with the olive oil inside. Transfer the egg mixture in the pressure cooker. Sprinkle it with the chopped parsley and close the lid. Cook the frittata for 10 minutes at the mode to" Steam." When the time is cooked, let cooked, let the dish cool little and serve.

Nutrition: calories 193, fat 14, fiber 1.4, carbs 4.2, protein 13.5

Breakfast Yogurt

Prep time: 10 minutes| **Cook time:** 30 minutes| **Servings:** 6

Ingredients:

- 8 cups almond milk
- 2 tablespoons plain Greek yogurt

Directions:

Pour the almond milk in the pressure cooker and close the lid. Set the pressure cooker mode to "Slow Cook," and cook the milk for 30 minutes or until it is reached 380 degrees Fahrenheit. Remove the milk from the pressure cooker and chill it until it reaches 100 F. Add the plain Greek yogurt and blend well. Let the mixture chill in the refrigerator overnight. Stir the yogurt carefully using a wooden spoon and transfer it to serving bowls.

Nutrition: calories 82, fat 3.4, fiber 0, carbs 10.8, protein 1.4

Breakfast Strata

Prep time: 10 minutes| **Cook time:** 15 minutes| **Servings:** 6

Ingredients:

- 6 slices keto bread
- 1 tablespoon mustard
- 1 teaspoon salt
- ½ cup parsley
- ¼ cup dill
- 1 cup cream
- 4 eggs
- 1 cup spinach
- 2 tablespoons butter

Directions:

Cut the keto bread into the cubes. Transfer the half of the bread in the pressure cooker. Whisk the eggs in the mixing bowl and add the salt, mustard, and cream. Chop the spinach and parsley. Add the chopped greens in the egg mixture. Add butter and whisk the mixture. Pour half of the egg mixture in the pressure cooker, and cover the dish with the remaining bread. Add the second part of the egg mixture. Close the lid, and set the pressure cooker mode to "Steam." Cook for 15 minutes. When the dish is cooked, allow it to cool briefly and transfer the dish to the serving plate. Cut it into pieces and serve.

Nutrition: calories 171, fat 10.3, fiber 3.2, carbs 11.9, protein 9.9

Egg Balls

Prep time: 15 minutes| **Cook time:** 30 minutes| **Servings:** 5

Ingredients:

- 5 eggs, boiled
- 1 cup ground chicken
- 1 teaspoon salt
- 1 teaspoon ground black pepper

- ½ cup pork rinds
- 1 teaspoon butter
- ½ teaspoon tomato paste
- 2 tablespoons almond flour
- 1 teaspoon oregano

Directions:

Peel the eggs. Combine the ground chicken, salt, ground black pepper, tomato paste, and oregano together in a mixing bowl. Blend the mixture well. Make the balls from the ground chicken mixture and flatten them. Put the peeled eggs in the middle of the ball and roll the meat mixture around them. Dip each one of them in the almond flour and pork rinds. Add the butter in the pressure cooker and transfer the egg's balls. Close the lid, and set the pressure cooker mode to "Sauté." Cook for 30 minutes. Open the pressure cooker during the cooking to turn the balls. When the egg balls are cooked, remove them from the pressure cooker and rest briefly. Serve immediately.

Nutrition: calories 237, fat 15.8, fiber 1.5, carbs 3.3, protein 21.6

Broccoli Rice

Prep time: 10 minutes| **Cook time:** 15 minutes| **Servings:** 4

Ingredients:

- 2 cup of broccoli rice
- 4 cups of water
- 1 tablespoon salt
- 3 tablespoons heavy cream

Directions:

Combine the broccoli rice, salt, and water together in the pressure cooker. Add cream. Stir the mixture gently and close the lid. Cook for 15 minutes on the mode to "Slow Cook." When the broccoli rice is cooked, remove it from the pressure cooker and rest briefly. Transfer the dish to the serving bowl. Serve the dish only warm.

Nutrition: calories 54, fat 4.3, fiber 1.2, carbs 3.3, protein 1.5

Spinach Muffins

Prep time: 10 minutes| **Cook time:** 8 minutes| **Servings:** 5

Ingredients:

- 2 cup spinach, chopped
- 5 eggs, whisked
- 1 tablespoon flax meal
- ½ teaspoon salt
- 1 teaspoon turmeric
- ½ teaspoon butter
- 1 cup water, for cooking

Directions:

In the mixing bowl mix up together chopped spinach, whisked eggs, flax meal, salt, turmeric, and butter. Transfer the mixture into the muffin molds. Pour water in the cooker and insert trivet. Place muffin molds on the trivet and close the lid. Cook muffins for 8 minutes on High-pressure mode. Then use quick pressure release. Chill the muffins until warm and remove from the muffin molds.

Nutrition: calories 77, fat 5.3, fiber 0.8, carbs 1.5, protein 6.2

Sweet Egg Toasts

Prep time: 10 minutes| **Cook time:** 8 minutes| **Servings:** 7

Ingredients:

- 4 eggs
- 1 cup of coconut milk
- 3 tablespoons Erythritol
- 1 teaspoon vanilla extract
- 1 tablespoon butter
- 7 slices carb bread

Directions:

Beat the eggs in the mixing bowl and add coconut milk. Whisk the mixture well and add

Erythritol. Sprinkle the egg mixture with the vanilla extract and stir. Dip the bread slices into the egg mixture. Add the butter in the pressure cooker. Add the dipped bread slices and close the lid. Set the pressure cooker mode to "Sauté," and cook for 4 minutes on each side. When the toasts are cooked, remove them from the pressure cooker and rest briefly before serving.

Nutrition: calories 175, fat 12.3, fiber 2.8, carbs 9.2, protein 8

Seeds Mix

Prep time: 10 minutes| **Cook time:** 25 minutes| **Servings:** 6

Ingredients:

- ½ cup flax seeds
- ½ cup flax meal
- ½ cup sunflower seeds
- 1 tablespoon tahini paste
- 3 cups chicken stock
- 1 teaspoon salt
- 1 onion, diced
- 3 tablespoons butter
- 3 ounces dates

Directions:

Combine flax seeds, flax meal, and sunflower seeds together in a mixing bowl. Add salt and diced onion. Chop the dates and add them to the mixture. Transfer the mixture in the pressure cooker and add chicken stock. Blend the mixture and close the lid. Set the pressure cooker mode to "Slow Cook," and cook for 25 minutes. When the cooking time ends, remove the mixture from the pressure cooker, and transfer it to a mixing bowl. Add butter and stir. Transfer the dish to serving plates.

Nutrition: calories 230, fat 15.7, fiber 7.3, carbs 19.4, protein 5.9

Zucchini Pasta with Chicken

Prep time: 10 minutes| **Cook time:** 25 minutes| **Servings:** 5

Ingredients:

- 1 zucchini
- 1 cup ground chicken
- ½ cup cream
- ½ cup chicken stock
- 1 teaspoon salt
- 1 teaspoon ground black pepper
- 1 teaspoon paprika
- ½ teaspoon ground coriander
- 1 teaspoon cilantro
- 1 onion

Directions:

Wash the zucchini and peel the onion. Grate the vegetables and combine them together in a mixing bowl. Add ground chicken, cream chicken stock, salt, ground black pepper, paprika, ground coriander, and cilantro. Blend the mixture well, and transfer it to the pressure cooker. Close the lid, and set the pressure cooker mode to «Sear/sauté.» Cook for 25 minutes. Open the pressure cooker lid and stir. Transfer the dish to the serving bowl and chill well.

Nutrition: calories 87, fat 3.6, fiber 1.2, carbs 4.7, protein 9.2

Breakfast Pasta Casserole

Prep time: 10 minutes| **Cook time:** 20 minutes| **Servings:** 6

Ingredients:

- 6 ounces Palmini pasta, cooked
- 8 ounces Romano cheese
- 1 cup cream
- 3 tablespoons butter
- 1 teaspoon salt
- 1 teaspoon paprika

- 1 teaspoon turmeric
- 1 cup parsley
- 1 teaspoon cilantro

Directions:

Grate the cheese. Place pasta in the pressure cooker. Sprinkle it with half of the cheese. Chop the parsley and add it in the pressure cooker mixture. Season the mixture with the salt, paprika, turmeric, and cilantro. Sprinkle the casserole with the remaining cheese. Add the butter and cream and close the lid. Set the pressure cooker mode to "Pressure," and cook for 20 minutes. When the casserole is cooked, remove it from the pressure cooker and cut into serving pieces.

Nutrition: calories 256, fat 18.5, fiber 1.9, carbs 6.7, protein 17.5

Egg Sandwiches

Prep time: 10 minutes| **Cook time:** 10 minutes| **Servings:** 4

Ingredients:

- 8 slices keto bread
- 6 ounces ham
- 6 ounces cheddar cheese
- 1 tablespoon mustard
- 4 eggs
- 1 tablespoon mayonnaise
- 1 teaspoon basil
- 1 teaspoon cilantro
- ½ teaspoon ground black pepper
- 1 teaspoon paprika

Directions:

Slice the ham and cheddar cheese. Combine the mayonnaise, basil, cilantro, ground black pepper, and paprika together in a mixing bowl. Add mustard and stir the mixture well. Spread every slice of bread with the mayonnaise mixture. Add ham and cheddar cheese on the four of the bread pieces and cover that with the remaining bread pieces. Whisk the eggs carefully, and dip the sandwiches in the egg mixture. Transfer the sandwiches to the pressure cooker and close the lid. Set the pressure cooker mode to "Sauté," and cook for 10 minutes. When the cooking time ends, remove the dish from the pressure cooker and serve immediately.

Nutrition: calories 399, fat 23.3, fiber 4.9, carbs 17.5, protein 31.3

Chicken Quiche

Prep time: 10 minutes| **Cook time:** 30 minutes| **Servings:** 6

Ingredients:

- 1 pound chicken
- 1 cup dill
- 2 eggs
- 8 ounces dough
- 1 teaspoon salt
- ½ teaspoon nutmeg
- 9 ounces cheddar cheese
- ½ cup cream
- 1 teaspoon oregano
- 1 teaspoon olive oil

Directions:

Chop the chicken and season it with the salt, oregano, and nutmeg. Blend the mixture. Chop the dill and combine it with the chopped chicken. Grate cheddar cheese. Take the round pie pan and spray it with the olive oil inside. Transfer the yeast dough into the pan and flatten it well. Add the chicken mixture. Whisk the eggs and add them to the quiche. Sprinkle it with the grated cheese and add cream. Transfer the quiche to the pressure cooker and close the lid. Set the pressure cooker mode to "Sauté," and cook for 30 minutes. When the cooking time ends, remove the dish from the pressure cooker and chill it well. Cut the quiche into slices and serve it.

Nutrition: calories 320, fat 14.1, fiber 3, carbs 13.65, protein 34

Zucchini Scramble

Prep time: 10 minutes| **Cook time:** 6 minutes| **Servings:** 2

Ingredients:

- ½ zucchini, grated
- 2 eggs, whisked
- 1 teaspoon butter
- ¼ cup cream
- 1 teaspoon ground black pepper

Directions:

Preheat cooker on Saute mode and toss butter. Melt it and add grated zucchini. Sprinkle the vegetables with ground black pepper and cream. Stir well. Cook them for 3 minutes. Then add whisked eggs and cook for 1 minute. Scramble eggs and cook them for 2 minutes more. Close the cooker and switch off it. Let the scramble rest for 10 minutes.

Nutrition: calories 110, fat 8.1, fiber 0.8, carbs 3.6, protein 6.5

Chocolate Slow Cook

Prep time: 10 minutes| **Cook time:** 13 minutes| **Servings:** 3

Ingredients:

- 1 cup flax meal
- 3 tablespoons cocoa powder
- 1 tablespoon Erythritol
- 1 teaspoon vanilla extract
- 1 cup of water
- ⅓ cup of coconut milk
- 1 tablespoon dark chocolate
- 1 tablespoon butter
- 1 teaspoon sesame seeds
- 3 tablespoons almonds
- 1 teaspoon raisins
- 1 teaspoon olive oil

Directions:

Crush the almonds. Combine the cocoa powder, Erythritol, vanilla extract, and chocolate together in a bowl and stir the mixture. Spray the pressure cooker with olive oil. Put the flax meal in the pressure cooker and add cocoa powder mixture. Add the crushed almonds, raisins, coconut milk, and water. Blend the mixture using a wooden spoon. Close the pressure cooker lid, and set the mode to "Pressure." Cook for 13 minutes. When the cooking time ends, mix up the Slow Cook carefully using a spoon until smooth. Transfer the cooked chocolate Slow Cook to serving bowls and serve.

Nutrition: calories 347, fat 30.3, fiber 13.9, carbs 19.7, protein 11.4

Cauliflower Rice Balls

Prep time: 10 minutes| **Cook time:** 15 minutes| **Servings:** 4

Ingredients:

- 1 cup cauliflower rice, cooked
- 2 eggs
- 1 carrot
- 1 white onion
- 1 teaspoon salt
- 3 tablespoons almond meal
- 1 tablespoon butter
- ⅓ cup ground chicken

Directions:

Peel the carrot and onion. Grate the vegetables and combine them in a mixing bowl. Add salt, almond meal, and ground chicken. Mix it up. Make the medium balls. Add the butter in the pressure cooker and add the balls. Close the pressure cooker lid, and set the pressure cooker mode to "Steam." Cook for 15 minutes. When the cooking time ends, let the dish rest briefly. Serve the balls warm.

Nutrition: calories 128, fat 8.2, fiber 2.2, carbs 6.5, protein 8.1

Coconut Porridge with Cream

Prep time: 10 minutes| **Cook time:** 20 minutes| **Servings:** 5

Ingredients:

- 1 cup chia seeds
- ⅓ cup raisins
- ½ cup coconut cream
- 2 tablespoons butter
- ½ teaspoon ground ginger
- 1 teaspoon vanilla extract
- 1 cup almond milk
- 2 tablespoons Erythritol

Directions:

Combine the coconut cream and almond milk together, and add ground ginger, vanilla extract, and Erythritol. Stir the mixture well. Add the butter and stir the mixture again. Chop the raisins. Transfer the coconut cream mixture in the pressure cooker. Add chia seeds and chopped fruit. Stir it. Close the lid, and set the pressure cooker mode to "Slow Cook." Cook for 15 minutes. When the porridge is cooked, open the pressure cooker lid and stir the dish gently. Transfer the dish to the serving bowls.

Nutrition: calories 266, fat 19.1, fiber 10.7, carbs 21.2, protein 5.6

Cottage Cheese Soufflé

Prep time: 10 minutes| **Cook time:** 45 minutes| **Servings:** 4

Ingredients:

- 8 ounces of cottage cheese
- 4 eggs
- ½ cup cream
- 4 tablespoons butter
- 3 tablespoons Erythritol
- 1 teaspoon vanilla extract

Directions:

Pour the cream into the pressure cooker basket and close the lid. Set the pressure cooker mode to "Slow Cook," and cook the dish until the cream rich the temperature of 180 F (approximately 20 minutes). Meanwhile, combine the cottage cheese and eggs together. Add Erythritol, vanilla extract, and butter. Blend the mixture using a hand blender. Add the cottage cheese mixture in the preheated cream mixture. Stir it carefully until smooth. Close the lid and cook the dish on the yogurt mode for 25 minutes. Remove the dish from the pressure cooker and rest briefly. Serve the soufflé warm.

Nutrition: calories 362, fat 28.3, fiber 0, carbs 12.99, protein 14

Creamy Porridge

Prep time: 5 minutes| **Cook time:** 10 minutes| **Servings:** 6

Ingredients:

- 1 cup chia seeds
- 1 cup sesame seeds
- 2 cups of coconut milk
- 1 teaspoon salt
- 3 tablespoons Erythritol
- ½ teaspoon vanilla extract
- 3 tablespoons butter
- 1 teaspoon clove
- ½ teaspoon turmeric

Directions:

Combine the coconut milk, salt, Erythritol, vanilla extract, clove, and turmeric together in the pressure cooker. Blend the mixture. Close the lid, and set the pressure cooker mode to "Pressure." Cook the liquid for 10 minutes. Open the lid and add chia seeds and sesame seeds. Stir the mixture well and close the lid. Cook for 2 minutes. Remove the dish from the pressure cooker and let it chill briefly before serving.

Nutrition: calories 467, fat 42.6, fiber 11.2, carbs 18.4, protein 9.3

Cauliflower Balls

Prep time: 10 minutes| **Cook time:** 20 minutes| **Servings:** 4

Ingredients:

- 1 pound cauliflower
- 1 white onion
- 3 tablespoons coconut flour
- 1 teaspoon olive oil
- ¼ cup tomato juice
- 1 teaspoon salt
- 2 tablespoons flax meal
- 1 teaspoon chicken stock
- 2 eggs

Directions:

Chop the cauliflower roughly and transfer it to a blender. Peel the onion and chop it. Transfer the chopped onion in a blender. Add the flax meal and eggs to a blender and blend on high until smooth. Remove the mixture from a blender and add chicken stock, salt, and flour. Knead the smooth cauliflower dough. Make the small balls from the cauliflower mixture and transfer them to the pressure cooker. Add tomato juice and close the lid. Set the pressure cooker mode to "Steam," and cook for 20 minutes. When the cooking time ends, unplug the pressure cooker and leave the cauliflower balls to rest for 10 minutes. Remove the dish from the pressure cooker and transfer it to serving plates.

Nutrition: calories 121, fat 5.3, fiber 6.7, carbs 14.1, protein 6.9

Cinnamon Chia Pudding

Prep time: 10 minutes| **Cook time:** 15 minutes| **Servings:** 4

Ingredients:

- 1 cup chia seeds
- 4 tablespoons Erythritol
- 2 cups of coconut milk
- 2 tablespoons heavy cream
- 1 teaspoon butter
- 1 teaspoon cinnamon
- 1 teaspoon ground cardamom

Directions:

Combine the chia seeds, Erythritol, and coconut milk together in the pressure cooker. Stir the mixture gently and close the lid. Set the pressure cooker mode to "Slow Cook," and cook for 10 minutes. When the cooking time ends, let the chia seeds rest little. Open the pressure cooker lid and add cream, cinnamon, cardamom, and butter. Blend the mixture well using a wooden spoon. Transfer the pudding to the serving bowls. Add cherry jam, if desired, and serve.

Nutrition: calories 486, fat 43.3, fiber 15.3, carbs 22.6, protein 8.8

Creamy Pumpkin Puree

Prep time: 10 minutes| **Cook time:** 20 minutes| **Servings:** 5

Ingredients:

- ¼ cup raisins
- pound pumpkin
- ½ cup of water
- 1 teaspoon butter
- tablespoons heavy cream
- 1 teaspoon cinnamon
- ½ teaspoon vanilla extract
- 1 tablespoon liquid stevia

Directions:

Peel the pumpkin and chop it. Transfer the chopped pumpkin in the pressure cooker. Add water, butter, cinnamon, and vanilla extract. Close the lid and cook for 20 minutes at the pressure cooker mode to "Pressure". When the cooking time ends, remove the mixture from the pressure cooker, and transfer it to a blender. Blend it well until smooth. Add raisins and cream and stir mixture well. Add liquid stevia and stir it again. Chill the puree briefly and serve.

Nutrition: calories 82, fat 3.3, fiber 3.1, carbs 13.7, protein 1.4

Bread Pudding

Prep time: 10 minutes| **Cook time:** 30 minutes| **Servings:** 7

Ingredients:

- 1 cup cream
- ½ cup of coconut milk
- 10 slices low carb bread
- 2 tablespoons butter
- 1 teaspoon vanilla extract
- 3 eggs
- 1 teaspoon salt
- 4 tablespoons stevia powder

Directions:

Chop the bread in the medium cubes and transfer it to the pressure cooker. Combine the coconut milk and cream together. Add eggs and whisk the mixture using a hand mixer. Add the vanilla extract, salt, and stevia. Stir the mixture well. Pour the mixture in the pressure cooker and close the lid. Leave the mixture for 15 minutes to let the bread absorb the coconut milk liquid. Set the pressure cooker mode to "Pressure," and cook for 30 minutes. When the cooking time ends, open the pressure cooker lid and let the pudding rest. Transfer the dish to serving plates.

Nutrition: calories 255, fat 15.4, fiber 6.1, carbs 13.7, protein 17.4

Creamy Mac Cups

Prep time: 10 minutes| **Cook time:** 25 minutes| **Servings:** 6

Ingredients:

- 8 ounces cauliflower, chopped
- 1 cup cream
- 1 cup of water
- 3 tablespoons butter
- 1 teaspoon salt
- 1 teaspoon basil
- 6 ounces Romano cheese
- 1 teaspoon paprika
- 1 teaspoon turmeric
- 3 ounces ham

Directions:

Coat six ramekins with butter. Combine the cauliflower, cream, and water together in a mixing bowl. Add salt, basil, paprika, and turmeric. Chop the ham and Romano cheese. Add the chopped ingredients in the cauliflower mixture and stir it well. Separate the cauliflower mixture between all ramekins and transfer the ramekins to the pressure cooker. Close the lid, and set the pressure cooker mode to "Steam." Cook for 25 minutes. When the dish is cooked, it should have a creamy, soft mixture, then let it cool briefly and serve.

Nutrition: calories 221, fat 17, fiber 1.3, carbs 5.3, protein 12.6

Scotch Eggs

Prep time: 15 minutes| **Cook time:** 30 minutes| **Servings:** 4

Ingredients:

- 4 eggs, boiled
- 1 cup ground beef
- 1 teaspoon salt
- 1 teaspoon turmeric
- 1 teaspoon cilantro
- ½ teaspoon ground black pepper
- ½ teaspoon butter
- 1 tablespoon lemon juice
- ½ teaspoon lime zest
- 1 tablespoon almond flour
- ⅓ cup pork rinds

- ¼ cup cream

Directions:

Peel the eggs. Combine the ground beef, salt, turmeric, cilantro, ground black pepper, lemon juice, and lime zest together. Stir the mixture well. Make the medium balls from the meat mixture and flatten them well. But the peeled eggs in the middle of the flatten balls and roll them. Dip the balls in the almond flour. Dip the meatballs in the cream and sprinkle them with the pork rind. Transfer the balls to the pressure cooker and close the lid. Set the pressure cooker mode to "Sauté," and cook for 30 minutes. When the cooking time ends, remove the scotch eggs from the pressure cooker carefully and serve immediately.

Nutrition: calories 230, fat 13, fiber 0.4, carbs 1.8, protein 25.8

Flax Meal with Almonds

Prep time: 10 minutes| **Cook time:** 7 minutes| **Servings:** 3

Ingredients:

- 1 cup flax meal
- 3 cups of coconut milk
- 2 tablespoons Erythritol
- 1 teaspoon vanilla extract
- 3 tablespoons almond flakes
- ½ teaspoon cinnamon
- ½ teaspoon nutmeg

Directions:

Put the flax meal in the pressure cooker and add coconut milk. Sprinkle the mixture with Erythritol, vanilla extract, cinnamon, and nutmeg. Blend the mixture well until smooth. Close the pressure cooker lid, and set the pressure cooker mode to "Slow Cook." Cook for 7 minutes. Open the pressure cooker lid and stir the Slow Cook carefully. Transfer it to serving bowls and sprinkle with the almond flakes.

Nutrition: calories 739, fat 72.4, fiber 16.6, carbs 25, protein 14.2

Chapter 2: Snacks and Appetizers Recipes

Zucchini Tots

Prep time: 15 minutes| **Cook time:** 9 minutes| **Servings:** 8

Ingredients

- 2 medium zucchinis
- 1 egg
- 1 teaspoon salt
- ½ teaspoon baking soda
- 1 teaspoon lemon juice
- 1 teaspoon basil
- 1 tablespoon oregano
- ⅓ cup oatmeal flour
- 1 tablespoon olive oil
- 1 teaspoon minced garlic
- 1 tablespoon butter

Directions:

Wash the zucchini and grate it. Beat the egg in a mixing bowl and blend it using a whisk. Add the baking soda, lemon juice, basil, oregano, and flour in the egg mixture. Stir it carefully until smooth. Combine the grated zucchini and egg mixture together. Knead the dough until smooth. Combine the olive oil and minced garlic together. Set the pressure cooker to "Sauté" mode. Add butter and transfer the mixture to the pressure cooker. Melt the mixture. Make the small tots from the zucchini dough and place them in the melted butter mixture. Sauté the dish for 3 minutes on each side. When the zucchini tots are cooked, remove them from the pressure cooker and serve.

Nutrition: calories 64, fat 4.4, fiber 0, carbs 4.35, protein 2

Shallot Pancakes

Prep time: 10 minutes| **Cook time:** 15 minutes| **Servings:** 8

Ingredients

- 8 ounces shallot
- 2 tablespoons chives
- 1 red onion
- 1 cup coconut flour
- 2 egg
- ¼ cup sour cream
- 1 teaspoon baking soda
- 1 tablespoon lemon juice
- 1 teaspoon salt
- 1 teaspoon cilantro
- ½ teaspoon basil
- 1 tablespoon olive oil
- 1 bell pepper

Directions:

Chop the shallot and chives and combine them into a mixing bowl. Peel the onion, dice it, and add it to the mixing bowl. Whisk the eggs in the separate bowl and add baking soda and lemon juice. Stir the mixture and add the cream, salt, cilantro, basil, and coconut flour. Blend the mixture well until smooth. Remove the seeds from the bell pepper and chop it into the tiny pieces. Add the vegetables to the egg mixture. Stir it to the batter that forms. Set the pressure cooker to "Sauté" mode. Pour the olive oil in the pressure cooker and preheat it. Ladle the batter and cook the pancakes for 2 minutes on each side. Keep the pancakes under aluminum foil to keep them warm until all the pancakes are cooked. Serve the pancakes while warm.

Nutrition: calories 138, fat 6, fiber 6.5, carbs 17.6, protein 4.7

Zucchini Muffins with Poppy Seeds

Prep time: 15 minutes| **Cook time:** 15 minutes| **Servings:** 6

Ingredients

- 1 cup coconut flour
- 1 medium zucchini
- 1 teaspoon baking soda
- 1 tablespoon lemon juice
- ½ teaspoon salt
- ½ teaspoon ground black pepper
- 1 tablespoon butter
- ⅓ cup of coconut milk
- 1 teaspoon poppy seeds
- 2 tablespoons flax meal

Directions:

Wash the zucchini and chop it roughly. Place the chopped zucchini in a blender and mix until smooth. Combine the salt, baking soda, lemon juice, poppy, coconut flour, butter, ground black pepper, and flax meal together. Add the milk and blended zucchini. Knead the dough until smooth. It can be a little bit sticky. Place the muffins in the muffin's tins and transfer the zucchini muffins in the pressure cooker. Cook the muffins on the "Steam" mode for 15 minutes. When the cooking time ends, check if the dish is cooked using a toothpick. If the muffins are cooked, remove them from the pressure cooker and serve.

Nutrition: calories 146, fat 8.9, fiber 8.1, carbs 13.5, protein 4

Deviled Eggs

Prep time: 10 minutes| **Cook time:** 5 minutes| **Servings:** 6

Ingredients

- 6 eggs
- 1 avocado, peeled
- 1 tablespoon cream
- ½ teaspoon minced garlic
- 1 cup water, for cooking

Directions:

Place the eggs in the Pressure cooker and add water. Close and seal the lid. Cook the eggs on High-pressure mode for 5 minutes. Then use natural pressure release for 5 minutes more. After this, blend together avocado, minced garlic, and cream. When the mixture is smooth, transfer it in the mixing bowl. Peel the cooked eggs and cut them into the halves. Remove the eggs yolks and transfer them in the avocado mixture. Stir well. Fill the egg whites with the avocado mixture.

Nutrition: calories 133, fat 11, fiber 2.2, carbs 3.4, protein 6.2

Herbed Butter

Prep time: 10 minutes| **Cook time:** 5 minutes| **Servings:** 7

Ingredients

- 1 cup butter
- 1 teaspoon minced garlic
- 1 teaspoon dried oregano
- 1 teaspoon dried cilantro
- 1 tablespoon dried dill
- 1 teaspoon salt
- ½ teaspoon ground black pepper

Directions:

Set Saute mode and place butter inside the Pressure cooker. Add minced garlic, dried oregano, dried cilantro, butter, dried dill, salt, and ground black pepper. Stir the mixture well and saute it for 4-5 minutes or until the butter is melted. Then switch off the cooker and stir the butter well. Transfer the butter mixture into the butter mold and freeze it.

Nutrition: calories 235, fat 26.3, fiber 0.2, carbs 0.6, protein 0.4

Broccoli Tots

Prep time: 15 minutes| **Cook time:** 8 minutes| **Servings:** 8

Ingredients

- 1 pound broccoli
- 3 cups of water
- 1 teaspoon salt
- 1 egg
- 1 cup pork rind
- ½ teaspoon paprika
- 1 tablespoon turmeric
- ⅓ cup almond flour
- 2 tablespoons olive oil

Directions:

Wash the broccoli and chop it roughly. Put the broccoli in the pressure cooker and add water. Set the pressure cooker to "Steam" mode and steam the broccoli for 20 minutes. Remove the broccoli from the pressure cooker and let it cool. Transfer the broccoli to a blender. Add egg, salt, paprika, turmeric, and almond flour. Blend the mixture until smooth. Add pork rind and blend the broccoli mixture for 1 minute more. Pour the olive oil in the pressure cooker. Form the medium tots from the broccoli mixture and transfer them to the pressure cooker. Set the pressure cooker to "Sauté" mode and cook for 4 minutes on each side. When the dish is cooked, remove the broccoli tots from the pressure cooker and allow them to rest before serving.

Nutrition: calories 147, fat 9.9, fiber 1.8, carbs 4.7, protein 11.6

Glazed Walnuts

Prep time: 5 minutes| **Cook time:** 4 minutes| **Servings:** 4

Ingredients

- ⅓ cup of water
- 6 ounces walnuts
- 5 tablespoon Erythritol
- ½ teaspoon ground ginger
- 3 tablespoons psyllium husk powder

Directions:

Combine Erythritol and water together in a mixing bowl. Add ground ginger and stir the mixture until the sugar is dissolved. Transfer the walnuts in the pressure cooker and add sweet liquid. Close the pressure cooker lid and cook the dish on the "Pressure" mode for 4 minutes. Remove the walnuts from the pressure cooker. Dip the walnuts in the Psyllium husk powder and serve.

Nutrition: calories 286, fat 25.1, fiber 8.2, carbs 10.4, protein 10.3

Wrapped Halloumi Cheese

Prep time: 10 minutes| **Cook time:** 10 minutes| **Servings:** 8

Ingredients

- 1-pound halloumi cheese
- 8 oz bacon, sliced
- 1 teaspoon olive oil

Directions:

Cut the cheese into 8 sticks. Wrap every cheese stick into the sliced bacon and sprinkle with olive oil. Place the wrapped sticks in the cooker basket and lower the air fryer lid. Cook the snack for 4 minutes from each side. Serve it warm.

Nutrition: calories 365, fat 29.4, fiber 0, carbs 1.9, protein 22.7

Onion Rings

Prep time: 10 minutes| **Cook time:** 8 minutes| **Servings:** 7

Ingredients

- 1 cup coconut flour
- 1 teaspoon salt
- ½ teaspoon basil
- 1 teaspoon oregano

- ½ teaspoon cayenne pepper
- 3 eggs
- 5 medium white onions
- 3 tablespoons sesame oil

Directions:

Combine the coconut flour, salt, basil, oregano, and cayenne pepper together in a mixing bowl. Stir the coconut flour mixture gently. Add the eggs in a separate bowl and whisk them. Peel the onions and cut them into the thick rings. Separate the onion rings and dip them into the egg mixture. Pour the sesame oil in the pressure cooker. Preheat it on the "Pressure" mode. Dip the onion rings in the flour mixture. Transfer the onion rings to the pressure cooker. Sauté the onions for 2 minutes on each side. Transfer the cooked rings on the paper towel and rest briefly. Season with salt while hot and serve.

Nutrition: calories 180, fat 10.1, fiber 7.5, carbs 16.8, protein 5.6

Cheesy Bombs

Prep time: 10 minutes| **Cook time:** 10 minutes| **Servings:** 8

Ingredients

- 6 ounces puff pastry
- 1 teaspoon salt
- 8 ounces mozzarella pearls
- 1 egg
- ½ cup coconut flour
- ¼ cup of coconut milk
- ½ teaspoon oregano
- 2 tablespoons butter

Directions:

Roll the puff pastry using a rolling pin. Add the egg to a mixing bowl and blend it using a whisk. Add coconut milk and salt and whisk the mixture until the salt is dissolved. Cut the rolled puff pastry into medium-sized squares. Put a mozzarella pearl in the middle of every square and wrap the dough around each one to make the balls. Sprinkle the egg mixture with the oregano and mix well. Dip the puff pastry balls into the egg mixture, then dip the balls into the coconut flour. Add the butter in the pressure cooker and melt it. Place the puff pastry balls in the pressure cooker and close the lid. Cook the dish on the "Pressure" mode for 10 minutes. When the cooking time ends, release the pressure and open the pressure cooker lid. Transfer the dish to serving plates.

Nutrition: calories 269, fat 19.4, fiber 3, carbs 14.1, protein 8.5

Garlic Tomato Slices

Prep time: 10 minutes| **Cook time:** 5 minutes| **Servings:** 5

Ingredients

- 5 tomatoes
- ¼ cup chives
- ⅓ cup garlic clove
- ½ teaspoon salt
- ½ teaspoon ground black pepper
- 1 tablespoon olive oil
- 7 ounces Parmesan cheese

Directions:

Wash the tomatoes and slice them into thick slices. Place the sliced tomatoes in the pressure cooker. Chop the chives and grate the Parmesan cheese. Peel the garlic cloves and mince them. Combine the grated cheese and minced garlic and stir the mixture. Sprinkle the tomato slices with the chives, ground black pepper, and salt. Then sprinkle the sliced tomatoes with the cheese mixture. Close the lid and cook the dish on the "Pressure" mode for 5 minutes. When the cooking time ends, remove the tomatoes carefully and serve.

Nutrition: calories 224 fat 14, fiber 1, carbs 12.55, protein 13

Creamy Shallots with Mushrooms

Prep time: 15 minutes| **Cook time:** 30 minutes| **Servings:** 7

Ingredients

- 9 ounces shallot
- 8 ounces mushrooms
- ½ cup chicken stock
- 1 tablespoon paprika
- ½ tablespoon salt
- ¼ cup cream
- 1 teaspoon coriander
- ½ cup dill
- ½ cup parsley
- 1 tablespoon Erythritol

Directions:

Slice the shallot and chop the mushrooms. Combine the chicken stock, salt, paprika, cream, coriander, and Erythritol in a mixing bowl. Blend the mixture well. Chop the dill and parsley. Pour the cream mixture in the pressure cooker. Set the pressure cooker to "Sauté" mode and add sliced shallot and chopped mushrooms. Blend the mixture using a wooden spoon. Close the lid and sauté the mixture for 30 minutes. Chop the parsley and dill. When the dish is cooked, transfer it to serving plates. Sprinkle the cooked dish with the chopped parsley and dill. Do not stir again before serving it.

Nutrition: calories 52, fat 1, fiber 1.3, carbs 10.2, protein 3

Meatloaf

Prep time: 10 minutes| **Cook time:** 40 minutes| **Servings:** 9

Ingredients

- 2 cups ground beef
- 1 cup ground chicken
- 2 eggs
- 1 tablespoon salt
- 1 teaspoon ground black pepper
- ½ teaspoon paprika
- 1 tablespoon butter
- 1 teaspoon cilantro
- 1 tablespoon basil
- ¼ cup fresh dill

Directions:

Combine the ground chicken and ground beef together in a mixing bowl. Add egg, salt, ground black pepper, paprika, butter, and cilantro. Add the basil. Chop the dill and add it to the ground meat mixture and stir using your hands. Place the meat mixture on aluminum foil, shape into a loaf and wrap it. Place it in the pressure cooker. Close the pressure cooker lid and cook the dish on the "Sauté" mode for 40 minutes. When the cooking time ends, remove the meatloaf from the pressure cooker and let it rest. Remove from the foil, slice it, and serve.

Nutrition: calories 173, fat 11.5, fiber 0, carbs 0.81, protein 16

Glazed Jalapeno Slices

Prep time: 5 minutes| **Cook time:** 7 minutes| **Servings:** 10

Ingredients

- 8 ounces jalapeno pepper
- ¼ cup Erythritol
- 5 tablespoon water
- 2 tablespoons butter
- 1 teaspoon paprika

Directions:

Wash the jalapeno pepper and remove the seeds. Slice it into the thin circles. Sprinkle the sliced jalapeno pepper with the paprika and Erythritol. Blend the mixture. Put the butter into the pressure cooker and add water. Set the pressure cooker to "Sauté" mode. When the butter starts to melt, add the sliced jalapeno in the pressure cooker. Close the lid and sauté the dish for 7 minutes. When the cooking time ends, remove the dish from the pressure cooker. Cool it and serve.

Nutrition: calories 28, fat 2.5, fiber 0.7, carbs 7.5, protein 0.4

Cauliflower Fritters

Prep time: 15 minutes| **Cook time:** 13 minutes| **Servings:** 7

Ingredients

- 1 pound cauliflower
- 1 medium white onion
- 1 teaspoon salt
- ½ teaspoon ground white pepper
- 1 tablespoon sour cream
- 1 teaspoon turmeric
- ½ cup dill
- 1 teaspoon thyme
- 3 tablespoons almond flour
- 1 egg
- 2 tablespoons butter

Directions:

Wash the cauliflower and separate it into the florets. Chop the florets and place them in a blender. Peel the onion and dice it. Add the diced onion in a blender and blend the mixture. When you get the smooth texture, add salt, ground white pepper, sour cream, turmeric, dill, thyme, and almond flour. Add egg blend the mixture well until a smooth dough forms. Remove the cauliflower dough from a blender and form the medium balls. Flatten the balls a little. Set the pressure cooker to "Sauté" mode. Add the butter in the pressure cooker and melt it. Add the cauliflower fritters in the pressure cooker, and sauté them for 6 minutes. Flip them once. Cook the dish on "Sauté" stew mode for 7 minutes. When the cooking time ends, remove the fritters from the pressure cooker And serve immediately.

Nutrition: calories 143, fat 10.6, fiber 3.9, carbs 9.9, protein 5.6

Breadsticks

Prep time: 25 minutes| **Cook time:** 10 minutes| **Servings:** 8

Ingredients

- 1 teaspoon baking powder
- ½ teaspoon Erythritol
- ½ teaspoon salt
- 1 cup of warm water
- 2 cups almond flour
- 5 ounces Parmesan
- 1 tablespoon olive oil
- 1 teaspoon onion powder
- 1 teaspoon basil

Directions:

Combine the baking powder, Erythritol, and warm water in a mixing bowl. Stir the mixture well. Add the almond flour, onion powder, salt, and basil. Knead the dough until smooth. Separate dough into 10 pieces and make the long logs. Twist the logs in braids. Grate the Parmesan cheese. Place the twisted logs in the pressure cooker. Sprinkle them with the grated Parmesan cheese and olive oil, and close the lid. Cook the breadsticks at the "Pressure" mode for 10 minutes. When the cooking time ends, release the pressure and open the pressure cooker. Leave the breadsticks for 10 minutes to rest. Serve the breadsticks immediately or keep them in a sealed container.

Nutrition: calories 242, fat 18.9, fiber 3, carbs 2.7, protein 11.7

Veggie Nuggets

Prep time: 10 minutes| **Cook time:** 10 minutes| **Servings:** 8

Ingredients

- 8 ounces cauliflower
- 1 big red onion

- 2 carrots
- ½ cup almond flour
- ¼ cup pork rinds
- 2 eggs
- 1 teaspoon salt
- ½ teaspoon red pepper
- ⅓ teaspoon ground white pepper
- 1 tablespoon olive oil
- 1 teaspoon dried dill

Directions:

Peel the red onion and carrots. Chop the vegetables roughly and transfer them to the food processor. Wash the cauliflower and separate it into the florets. Add the cauliflower florets to a food processor and puree until smooth. Add the eggs and salt. Blend the mixture for 3 minutes. Remove the vegetable mixture from the food processor and add to a mixing bowl. Add pork rinds, red pepper, ground white pepper, and dill. Blend the mixture until smooth. Form the nuggets from the vegetable mixture and dip them in the almond flour. Spray the pressure cooker with olive oil inside. Place the vegetable nuggets in the pressure cooker and cook them on the "Sauté" mode for 10 minutes. Stir the dish frequently. When the nuggets are cooked, remove them from the pressure cooker and serve.

Nutrition: calories 85, fat 5.1, fiber 1.8, carbs 5.9, protein 5

Chicken Nuggets

Prep time: 15 minutes| **Cook time:** 20 minutes| **Servings:** 6

Ingredients

- 2 cups ground chicken
- ½ cup dill
- 1 egg
- 2 tablespoons pork rinds
- 1 tablespoon heavy cream
- ½ cup almond flour
- 3 tablespoons butter
- 1 tablespoon canola oil
- 1 teaspoon ground black pepper

Directions:

Wash the dill and chop it. Beat the egg in the mixing bowl and whisk it. Add the chopped dill and ground chicken. Blend the mixture until it is smooth. Sprinkle the dish with the ground black pepper and cream. Blend the nugget mixture again. Form the nuggets from the meat mixture and dip them in the almond flour and pork rinds. Sprinkle the pressure cooker with the canola oil and butter. Set the pressure cooker to "Pressure" mode. When the butter mixture starts to melt, add the nuggets. Close the pressure cooker lid and cook the dish for 20 minutes. When the cooking time ends, check if the nuggets are cooked and remove them from the pressure cooker. Drain on paper towel and serve.

Nutrition: calories 217, fat 15.4, fiber 0.9, carbs 3.1, protein 17.4

Carrot Spirals

Prep time: 10 minutes| **Cook time:** 13 minutes| **Servings:** 4

Ingredients

- 1 cup of water
- 4 big carrots
- 1 teaspoon liquid stevia
- 1 tablespoon turmeric
- 1 tablespoon butter
- ½ teaspoon ground ginger

Directions:

Wash and peel the carrots. Use a spiralizer to make the curls or spirals. Put the carrot spirals in the pressure cooker. Combine the liquid stevia, water, turmeric, and ground ginger together in a mixing bowl. Stir the mixture well. Set the pressure cooker to "Sauté" mode. Add the butter to the carrot mixture and sauté it for 3 minutes. Stir the vegetables frequently. Add the stevia mixture and close the lid. Cook the dish on "Sauté" mode for 10 minutes. When the carrot spirals are cooked, remove them from the pressure cooker, strain them from the stevia liquid, and serve.

Nutrition: calories 62, fat 3.1, fiber 2.2, carbs 8.3, protein 0.8

Stuffed Dates

Prep time: 5 minutes| **Cook time:** 7 minutes| **Servings:** 7

Ingredients

- 6 ounces Parmesan cheese
- 8 ounces dates, ripe
- 1 teaspoon minced garlic
- 1 tablespoon sour cream
- 1 teaspoon butter
- ½ teaspoon ground white pepper
- 1 teaspoon oregano

Directions:

Remove the stones from the dates. Combine the minced garlic, sour cream, ground white pepper, and oregano, and stir the mixture. Grate the Parmesan cheese, and add it to the minced garlic mixture. Blend the mixture until smooth. Stuff the dates with the cheese mixture and place the dish in the pressure cooker. Set the pressure cooker to "Pressure" mode Add butter and close the pressure cooker lid. Cook the dish for 7 minutes. When the cooking time ends, remove it from the pressure cooker, let it rest briefly, and serve.

Nutrition: calories 203, fat 7.6, fiber 3, carbs 28.35, protein 8

Dried Tomatoes

Prep time: 5 minutes| **Cook time:** 8 hours| **Servings:** 8

Ingredients

- 5 medium tomatoes
- 1 tablespoon basil
- 1 teaspoon cilantro
- 1 tablespoon onion powder
- 5 tablespoon olive oil
- 1 teaspoon paprika

Directions:

Wash the tomatoes and slice them. Combine the cilantro, basil, and paprika together and stir well. Place the sliced tomatoes in the pressure cooker and sprinkle them with the spice mixture. Add olive oil and close the lid. Cook the dish on the "Slow Cook" mode for 8 hours. When the cooking time ends, the tomatoes should be semi-dry. Remove them from the pressure cooker. Serve the dish warm or keep it in the refrigerator.

Nutrition: calories 92, fat 8.6, fiber 1, carbs 3.84, protein 1

Crunchy Chicken Skin

Prep time: 10 minutes| **Cook time:** 10 minutes| **Servings:** 7

Ingredients

- 1 teaspoon red chili flakes
- 1 teaspoon ground black pepper
- 1 teaspoon salt
- 9 ounces of chickens skin
- 2 tablespoons butter
- 1 teaspoon olive oil
- 1 teaspoon paprika

Directions:

Combine the ground black pepper, chili flakes, and paprika together. Stir the mixture and combine it with the chicken skin. Let the mixture rest for 5 minutes. Set the pressure cooker to "Sauté" mode. Add the butter in the pressure cooker and melt it. Add the chicken skin and sauté it for 10 minutes, stirring frequently. When the chicken skin gets crunchy, remove it from the pressure cooker. Place the chicken skin on the paper towel and drain. Serve warm.

Nutrition: calories 134, fat 11.5, fiber 0, carbs 0.98, protein 7

Gratin Mustard Potatoes

Prep time: 8 minutes| **Cook time:** 8 minutes| **Servings:** 6

Ingredients

- 3 tablespoons mustard
- 10 ounces red potatoes
- ½ cup dill
- 2 tablespoons butter
- 1 teaspoon salt
- 1 tablespoon minced garlic
- 1 teaspoon paprika
- 1 teaspoon cilantro
- 1 tablespoon oregano
- 4 tablespoons water

Directions:

Wash the potatoes and chop it into medium cubes with the skin on. Sprinkle the red potato cubes with the salt and oregano. Stir the mixture and place it in the pressure cooker. Add water and butter. Close the lid and cook the dish on the "Pressure" for 8 minutes. Chop the dill. Combine the mustard, minced garlic, paprika, cilantro, and chopped dill together. Stir the mixture well until smooth. When the red potato cubes are cooked, remove the dish from the pressure cooker. Transfer it to a serving bowl. Add butter, sprinkle the dish with the mustard sauce and serve.

Nutrition: calories 75, fat 4.2, fiber 1, carbs 8.7, protein 1

Cashew Cream

Prep time: 8 minutes| **Cook time:** 10 minutes| **Servings:** 10

Ingredients

- 3 cups cashew
- 2 cups chicken stock
- 1 teaspoon salt
- 1 tablespoon butter
- 2 tablespoons ricotta cheese

Directions:

Combine the cashews with the chicken stock in the pressure cooker. Add salt and close the pressure cooker lid. Cook the dish on the "Pressure" mode for 10 minutes. Remove the cashews from the pressure cooker and drain the nuts from the water. Transfer the cashews to a blender, and add the ricotta cheese and butter. Blend the mixture until it is smooth. When you get the texture you want, remove it from a blender. Serve it immediately or keep the cashew butter in the refrigerator.

Nutrition: calories 252, fat 20.6, fiber 1.2, carbs 13.8, protein 6.8

Chapter 3: Chicken and Poultry Recipes

Roasted Crisp Whole Chicken

Roasted chicken is a favorite to many because it is so sweet and this recipe is no exception! The lemon gives the recipe another good taste which improves the recipe!

Prep time: 10 minutes| **Cook time:** 25 minutes| **Servings:** 2

Ingredients:

- 1 whole Cornish Hen
- ½ tsp seasoned salt
- Juice of ½ lemon
- 1 tbsp honey
- ¼ cup hot water
- ¼ teaspoon salt
- ½ teaspoon whole peppercorns
- 1 sprigs of fresh thyme
- 2 cloves of garlic
- 1 tsp canola oil

Directions:

1. Combine lemon juice, honey, water, salt, peppercorns, thyme, and garlic in pot.
2. Season the chicken inside, outside and underneath the skin with seasoned salt.
3. Place the chicken in the air crisp basket then place into the pot.
4. Install pressure lid. Close pot, choose high, and cook for 15 minutes.
5. Once done cooking, do a quick release. Remove pressure lid.
6. Brush the chicken with canola oil
7. Close the crisping lid and select roast.
8. Set the time for 15 minutes and halfway through cooking time turn chicken over.
9. The juices in the bottom of the cooking pot make a delicious sauce.

Nutrition: Calories 196, Fats 6.3g, Carbs 10.5g, protein 24.2g

Glazed Chicken Drumsticks

Prep time: 15 mins | **Cook time:** 25 mins | **Servings:** 4

Ingredients:

- ¼ cup Dijon mustard
- 1 tablespoon honey
- 2 tablespoons olive oil
- Salt and ground black pepper, as required
- 4 (6 ounces) chicken drumsticks

Directions:

1. In a bowl, add all the ingredients except the drumsticks and mix until well combined.
2. Add the drumsticks and coat with the mixture generously.
3. Refrigerate, covered to marinate overnight.
4. In the pot of Ninja Foodi, place 1 cup of water.
5. Arrange the greased "Cook & Crisp Basket" in the pot of Ninja Foodi.
6. Place the chicken drumsticks into the "Cook & Crisp Basket."
7. Close the Ninja Foodi with the pressure lid and place the pressure valve to the "Seal" position.
8. Select "Pressure" and set it to "High" for 6 minutes.
9. Press "Start/Stop" to begin cooking.
10. Switch the valve to "Vent" and do a "Quick" release.
11. Now, close the Ninja Foodi with a crisping lid and Select "Air Crisp."
12. Set the temperature to 320 degrees F for 12 minutes.
13. Press "Start/Stop" to begin cooking.

14. After 12 minutes of cooking, set the temperature to 355 degrees F for 5 minutes.
15. Open the lid and serve hot.

Nutrition: Calories: 374, Fat: 17.3g, Saturated Fat: 3.6g, Trans Fat: 13.6g, Carbohydrates: 5.2g, Fiber 0.5g, Sodium 35mg, Protein: 47.5 g

Green Curry Chicken Thai Style

It has several but very amazing ingredients which make it deliciously spicy. The recipes include coconut milk, cumin powder, onion, Thai green curry paste and many others. It is finger licking good!

Prep time: 4 minutes| **Cook time:** 15 minutes| **Servings:** 2

Ingredients:

- 1 tablespoon Thai green curry paste
- 1|3 cup coconut milk
- ½ teaspoon coriander powder
- ½ teaspoon cumin powder
- 1|3-pound chicken breasts, bones removed and cut into chunks
- ¼ cup chicken broth
- 1 tablespoon fish sauce
- ¼ tablespoon sear button sugar
- ½ tablespoon lime juice
- 1 lime leaves, crushed
- ¼ cup bamboo shoots, sliced
- ¼ cup onion, cubed
- Salt and pepper to taste
- 1|3 cup green bell pepper
- 1|3 cup zucchini, sliced
- 2 tbsp Thai basil leaves

Directions:

1. Press the sauté button on the Ninja Foodi. Place the Thai green curry paste and the coconut milk. Stir until the mixture bubbles. Stir in the coriander and cumin powder and cook for 30 seconds.

2. Stir in the chicken and coconut broth. Season with fish sauce, sear button sugar, lime juice, bamboo shoots, lime leaves, and onion. Season with salt and pepper to taste.

3. Install pressure lid. Close Ninja Foodi, press the manual button, choose high settings, and set time to 10 minutes.

4. Once done cooking, do a quick release. Open the lid and press the sauté button. Stir in the green bell pepper, zucchini, and basil leaves. Allow to simmer for at least 5 minutes to cook the vegetables.

5. Serve and enjoy.

Nutrition: Calories 208, carbs 9 g, protein 16 g, fats 12g

Herbed Cornish Hen

Prep time: 15 mins| **Cook time:** 16 mins| **Servings:** 6

Ingredients:

- ½ cup olive oil
- 1 teaspoon fresh rosemary, chopped
- 1 teaspoon fresh thyme, chopped
- 1 teaspoon fresh lemon zest, grated finely
- ¼ teaspoon sugar
- ¼ teaspoon red pepper flakes, crushed
- Salt and ground black pepper, as required
- 2 pounds Cornish game hen, backbone removed and halved

Directions:

1. In a large bowl, mix well all ingredients except hen portions.

2. Add the hen portions and coat with marinade generously.

3. Cover and refrigerator for about 2-24 hours.

4. In a strainer, place the hen portions to drain any liquid.

5. Arrange the greased "Cook & Crisp Basket" in the pot of Ninja Foodi.

6. Close the Ninja Foodi with crisping lid and select "Air Crisp".
7. Set the temperature to 390 degrees F for 5 minutes.
8. Press "Start/Stop" to begin preheating.
9. After preheating, open the lid.
10. Place the hen portions into the "Cook & Crisp Basket".
11. Close the Ninja Foodi with crisping lid and select "Air Crisp".
12. Set the temperature to 390 degrees F for 16 minutes.
13. Press "Start/Stop" to begin cooking.
14. Open the lid and place the hen portions onto a cutting board.
15. Cut each portion in 2 pieces and serve hot.

Nutrition: Calories: 681, Fat: 57.4g, Saturated, Fat: 12.7g**,** Trans Fat: 44.7g, Carbohydrates: 0.8g**,** Fiber 0.3g, Sodium 180mg, Protein: 38.2g

Duck with Berries Mix

The Duck with Berries Mix is made using simple ingredients. It has all one can wish for in a nice meal. It is big in size and not like the small sizes served in restaurants. You will enjoy every bit of this amazing recipe!

Prep time: 10 minutes| **Cook time:** 25 minutes| **Servings:** 4

Ingredients:

- 1-pound duck breast, skinless, boneless, halved
- 2 tablespoons butter, melted
- 1 cup blackberries
- 1 teaspoon sweet paprika
- Salt and black pepper
- 1 cup chicken stock
- 2 spring onions, chopped
- 2 tablespoons cilantro, chopped

Directions:

1. Set the Foodi on Sauté mode, add the butter, heat it up, add the onion the meat and brown for 5 minutes.
2. Add the berries and the remaining ingredients, put the pressure lid on and cook on High for 20 minutes.
3. Release the pressure naturally for 10 minutes, divide the mix between plates and serve.

Nutrition: calories 319, fat 17.4g, carbs 11.4g, protein 15.9g

Garlic Duck and Apples

Garlic Duck and Apples is a simple meal that has lots of flavor. Can't forget to mention that it very nutritious!

Prep time: 10 minutes| **Cook time:** 30 minutes| **Servings:** 4

Ingredients:

- 2 duck legs, boneless
- 1 tablespoon avocado oil
- 2 garlic cloves, minced
- 1 tablespoon cilantro, chopped
- 2 apples, cored and cut into wedges
- ¾ cup white wine
- 1 teaspoon chili powder
- Salt and black pepper to the taste

Directions:

1. Put the reversible rack in the Foodi, add the baking pan and grease it with the oil.
2. Add the duck, the garlic and the other ingredients, set the machine on Baking mode and cook at 380 degrees F for 30 minutes.
3. Divide everything between plates and serve.

Nutrition: calories 170, fat 3g, carbs 17.7g, protein 11.5g

Traditional Chicken 'n Dumplings

The chicken 'n Dumplings, apart from being delicious it is also soft and eaten with ease. The tomatoes bring in the sweet flavor!

Prep time: 5 minutes | **Cook time:** 25 minutes | **Servings:** 2

Ingredients:

- 1-pound chicken breasts, cut into cubes
- 2 cloves of garlic, minced
- ½ cup chopped onion
- ½ cup chopped celery
- ½ teaspoon dried thyme
- ½ tablespoon bouillon
- 1 cup frozen vegetables, peas and carrots
- 1 ½ cups chicken stock
- 1 can cream, chicken
- Salt and pepper to taste
- ½ can southern homestyle biscuits
- 2 tbsp parsley, chopped

Directions:

1. Press the sauté button on the Ninja Foodi and stir in the chicken, garlic, onion, celery, and thyme. Stir constantly and allow the onions to sweat.

2. Stir in bouillon, vegetables, stock, and cream of chicken. Stir in the cream of chicken and season with salt and pepper to taste. Allow to simmer for a few minutes. Add the biscuits on top.

3. Install pressure lid. Close Ninja Foodi, press the pressure button, choose high settings, and set time to 15 minutes.

4. Once done cooking, do a quick release.

5. Remove pressure lid. Cover, press roast, and roast for 5 minutes at 400oF.

6. Garnish with parsley.

7. Serve and enjoy.

Nutrition: Calories 726; carbs 51.2g, protein 63.8g, fats 29.6g

Lemony Whole Chicken

Prep time: 15 mins | **Cook time:** 1 hour 29 minutes | **Servings:** 10

Ingredients:

- 1 (6-pound) whole chicken, necks and giblets removed
- Salt and ground black pepper, as required
- 3 fresh rosemary sprigs, divided
- 1 lemon, zested and cut into quarters
- 2 large onions, sliced,
- 4 cups chicken broth

Directions:

1. Stuff the cavity of chicken with 2 rosemary sprigs and lemon quarters.

2. Season the chicken with salt and black pepper evenly.

3. Chop the remaining rosemary sprig and set aside.

4. Select "Sauté/Sear" setting of Ninja Foodi and place the chicken into the pot.

5. Press "Start/Stop" to begin and cook, uncovered for about 5-7 minutes per side.

6. Remove chicken from the pot and place onto a roasting rack.

7. In the pot, place the onions and broth.

8. Arrange the "Reversible Rack" over the broth mixture.

9. Arrange the roasting rack on top of "Reversible Rack".

10. Sprinkle the chicken with reserved chopped rosemary and lemon zest.

11. Close the Ninja Foodi with crisping lid and select "Bake|Roast".

12. Set the temperature to 375 degrees F for 1¼ hours.

13. Press "Start/Stop" to begin cooking.

14. Open the lid and place the chicken onto a cutting board for about 10 minutes before carving.

15. Cut into desired sized pieces and serve.

Nutrition: Calories: 545, Fat: 20.8g, Saturated Fat: 5.7g, Trans Fat: 15.1g, Carbohydrates: 3.3g, Sodium 556mg, Protein: 81g

Turkey Potato Pie

This healthy and tasteful recipe is one of the easy go-to recipes. You will enjoy every bit of it!

Prep time: 10 minutes| **Cook time:** 26 minutes| **Servings:** 6

Ingredients:

- 1 onion, diced
- 2 garlic cloves, minced
- 2 pounds boneless turkey breasts, cut into 1-inch cubes
- 2 Yukon Gold potatoes, diced
- 1 cup chicken broth
- ½ stick unsalted butter
- ½ teaspoon sea salt
- ½ teaspoon black pepper
- 2 cups mixed vegetables of your choice
- ½ cup heavy, whipping cream
- 1 refrigerated piecrust

Directions:

1. Take Ninja Foodi multi-cooker, arrange it over a cooking platform, and open the top lid.
2. In the pot, add the butter; Select "sear/sauté" mode and select "md: hi" pressure level.
3. Press "stop/start." After about 4-5 minutes, the butter will start simmering.
4. Add the onion, garlic, and cook (while stirring) until it becomes softened and translucent for 2-3 minutes.
5. Add the turkey, potatoes, and broth; stir gently — season with the ground black pepper and salt.
6. Seal the multi-cooker by locking it with the pressure lid; ensure to keep the pressure release valve locked/sealed.
7. Select "pressure" mode and select the "hi" pressure level. Then, set timer to 10 minutes and press "stop/start"; it will start the cooking process by building up inside pressure.
8. When the timer goes off, quick release pressure by adjusting the pressure valve to the vent. After pressure gets released, open the pressure lid.
9. Select "sear/sauté" mode and select the "md" pressure level; add the cream and vegetables and combine. Stir-cook for 3 minutes to thicken the sauce.
10. In the pie crust, add the cooked mixture and fold the edges. Make a few cuts on top for steam escape.
11. Place the pie crust in the pot.
12. Seal the multi-cooker by locking it with the crisping lid; ensure to keep the pressure release valve locked/sealed.
13. Select "broil" mode and select the "hi" pressure level. Then, set timer to 10 minutes and press "stop/start"; it will start the cooking process by building up inside pressure.
14. When the timer goes off, quick release pressure by adjusting the pressure valve to the vent.
15. After pressure gets released, open the pressure lid.
16. Serve warm and enjoy!

Nutrition: Calories 653, Fats 29g, Carbs 43.5g, Protein 41g

Garlic Chicken in Creamy Tuscan Style

This is recipe is made full of flavor and made from ingredients that are addictive-free. It also contains all the nutrients that are needed for various body functions. Try it today!

Prep time: 5 minutes| **Cook time:** 15 minutes| **Servings:** 2

Ingredients:

- 1 tablespoon olive oil

- 1-pound skinless chicken breasts, halved, pounded
- 2 cloves, garlic, minced
- ½ tablespoon Italian seasoning
- ½ teaspoon salt
- 1|3 cup chicken stock
- 1|3 cup heavy cream
- 1|3 cup parmesan cheese
- ¼ cup sun-dried tomato

Directions:

1. Press the sauté button on the Ninja Foodi and sear the chicken breasts on all sides.
2. Stir in the garlic, Italian seasoning, and salt.
3. Pour in the chicken stock and the rest of the ingredients.
4. Install pressure lid. Close Ninja Foodi, press the pressure button, choose high settings, and set time to 10 minutes.
5. Once done cooking, do a quick release.
6. Serve and enjoy.

Nutrition: Calories 521; carbs 10.8g, protein 59.9g, fats 26.5g

Bacon-Wrapped Chicken Breasts

Prep time: 20 mins | **Cook time:** 20 mins | **Servings:** 4

Ingredients:

- 1 tablespoon sugar
- 8 fresh basil leaves
- 2 tablespoons red boat fish sauce
- 2 tablespoons water
- 2 (8-ounce) boneless chicken breasts, cut each breast in half horizontally
- Salt and ground black pepper, as required
- 8 bacon strips
- 1 tablespoon honey

Directions:

1. In a small heavy-bottomed pan, add the sugar over medium-low heat and cook for about 2-3 minutes or caramelized, stirring continuously.
2. Stir in the basil, fish sauce, and water.
3. Remove from heat and transfer into a large bowl.
4. Sprinkle the chicken with salt and black pepper.
5. Add the chicken pieces in the basil mixture and coat generously.
6. Refrigerate to marinate for about 4-6 hours.
7. Wrap each chicken piece with 2 bacon strips.
8. Coat each chicken piece with honey slightly.
9. Arrange the greased "Cook & Crisp Basket" in the pot of Ninja Foodi.
10. Close the Ninja Foodi with a crisping lid and select "Air Crisp."
11. Set the temperature to 365 degrees F for 5 minutes.
12. Press "Start/Stop" to begin preheating.
13. After preheating, open the lid.
14. Place the chicken breasts into the "Cook & Crisp Basket."
15. Close the Ninja Foodi with a crisping lid and select "Air Crisp."
16. Set the temperature to 365 degrees F for 20 minutes.
17. Press "Start/Stop" to begin cooking.
18. Open the lid and serve hot.

Nutrition: Calories: 564, Fat: 32.6g, Saturated Fat: 10.3g, Trans Fat: 22.3g, Carbohydrates: 8.2g, Fiber 0g, Sodium 2100mg, Protein: 56.3g

Spinach Stuffed Chicken Breasts

Prep time: 15 mins | **Cook time:** 30 mins | **Servings:** 2

Ingredients:

- 1 tablespoon olive oil
- 1¾ ounces fresh spinach
- ¼ cup ricotta cheese, shredded

- 2 (4-ounce) skinless, boneless chicken breasts
- Salt and ground black pepper, as required
- 2 tablespoons cheddar cheese, grated
- ¼ teaspoon paprika

Directions:

1. Select the "Sauté/Sear" setting of Ninja Foodi and place the oil into the pot.
2. Press "Start/Stop" to begin cooking and heat for about 2-3 minutes.
3. Add the spinach and cook for about 3-4 minutes.
4. Stir in the ricotta and cook for about 40-60 seconds.
5. Press "Start/Stop" to stop cooking and transfer the spinach mixture into a bowl.
6. Set aside to cool.
7. Cut slits into the chicken breasts about ¼-inch apart but not all the way through.
8. Stuff each chicken breast with the spinach mixture.
9. Sprinkle each chicken breast with salt and black pepper and then with cheddar cheese and paprika.
10. Arrange the greased "Cook & Crisp Basket" in the pot of Ninja Foodi.
11. Close the Ninja Foodi with a crisping lid and select "Air Crisp."
12. Set the temperature to 390 degrees F for 5 minutes.
13. Press "Start/Stop" to begin preheating.
14. After preheating, open the lid.
15. Place the chicken breasts into the "Cook & Crisp Basket."
16. Close the Ninja Foodi with a crisping lid and select "Air Crisp."
17. Set the temperature to 390 degrees F for 25 minutes.
18. Press "Start/Stop" to begin cooking.
19. Open the lid and serve hot.

Nutrition: Calories: 279, Fat: 16g, Saturated Fat: 5.6g, Trans Fat: 10.4g, Carbohydrates: 2.7g, Fiber 0.7g, Sodium 220mg, Protein: 31.4g

Tasty Sesame-Honeyed Chicken

Love chicken? If yes then this is one of the chicken recipes that you should not miss. It is so sweet and yummy!

Prep time: 4 minutes| **Cook time:** 16 minutes| **Servings:** 2

Ingredients:

- 1 tablespoon olive oil
- ½ onion, diced
- 2 cloves of garlic, minced
- 1-pound chicken breasts
- ¼ cup soy sauce
- 2 tbsp ketchup
- 1 tsp sesame oil
- ¼ cup honey
- ½ teaspoon red pepper flakes
- 1 tablespoon cornstarch + 1 ½ tablespoons water
- Green onions for garnish
- 1 tablespoon sesame seeds for garnish

Directions:

1. Press the sauté button on the Ninja Foodi and heat the oil. Stir in the onion and garlic until fragrant.
2. Add the chicken breasts. Allow to sear on all sides for three minutes.
3. Stir in the soy sauce, ketchup, sesame oil, honey, and red pepper flakes.
4. Install pressure lid. Close Ninja Foodi, press the pressure button, choose high settings, and set time to 10 minutes.
5. Once done cooking, do a quick release.
6. Open the lid and press the sauté button. Stir in the cornstarch slurry and allow to simmer until the sauce thickens.

7. Garnish with green onions and sesame seeds last.

8. Serve and enjoy.

Nutrition: Calories 568, Carbs 49.1g, protein 50.9g, fats 34.6g

Thyme Duck

This is one of the easiest recipes to make. It has only six ingredients and only takes only 30 minutes to be ready! It tastes so good and is a good treat for you and your guests.

Prep time: 10 minutes| **Cook time:** 30 minutes| **Servings:** 4

Ingredients:

- 2 duck legs, boneless, cubed
- 2 tablespoons butter, melted
- Salt and black pepper
- 1 teaspoon thyme, dried
- 1 cup tomatoes, halved
- 1 tablespoon parsley, chopped

Directions:

1. Set the Foodi on Sauté mode, add the oil, heat it up, add the meat and thyme and brown for 5 minutes.

2. Add the rest of the ingredients except the parsley, put the pressure lid on and cook on High for 25 minutes.

3. Release the pressure naturally for 10 minutes, divide the mix between plates, sprinkle the parsley on top and serve.

Nutrition: calories 127, fat 8.1g, carbs 2g, protein 11.4g

Hot Turkey Cutlets

It's a traditional bird that is usually enjoyed during holidays, especially Thanksgiving. There is much more to it than just its great taste. It has lots of proteins, way more than chicken and beef!

Prep time: 10 minutes| **Cook time:** 15 minutes| **Servings:** 4

Ingredients

- 1 teaspoon Greek seasoning
- 1-pound turkey cutlets
- 2 tablespoons olive oil
- 1 teaspoon turmeric powder
- ½ cup almond flour

Directions:

1. Take a bowl and add Greek seasoning, turmeric powder, almond flour and mix well

2. Dredge turkey cutlets in the bowl and let it sit for 30 minutes

3. Set your Ninja Foodi to Sauté mode and add oil, let it heat up

4. Add cutlets and Sauté for 2 minutes

5. Lock lid and cook on Low-Medium Pressure for 20 minutes

6. Release pressure naturally over 10 minutes

7. Take the dish out, serve and enjoy!

Nutrition: Calories: 340, Fats 19g, Carbs 3.7g, Protein 36g

Duck with Asparagus

This recipe is definitely so delicious just like many poultry recipes. It is so nutritious with protein, B vitamins, iron, zinc and iron from the duck legs.

Prep time: 5 minutes| **Cook time:** 25 minutes| **Servings:** 4

Ingredients:

- 2 duck legs, boneless
- 2 shallots, chopped
- 2 tablespoons butter
- 1 tablespoon sweet paprika
- 1 tablespoon tomato paste
- ½ cup chicken stock
- 1 bunch asparagus, trimmed, halved
- 1 tablespoon dill, chopped

Directions:

1. Set the Foodi on Sauté mode, add the butter, melt it, add the shallots and the duck and brown for 5 minutes.
2. add the rest of the ingredients, put the pressure lid on and cook on High for 20 minutes.
3. Release the pressure fast for 5 minutes, divide everything between plates and serve.

Nutrition: calories 254, fat 4.6g, carbs 18.4g, protein 30g

Savory 'n Aromatic Chicken Adobo

Do you love chicken? If yes to then this is the perfect meal for you because it brings in different flavors and the result is amazing! This recipe is spiced a little so as to give it more sweet taste!

Prep time: 5 minutes| **Cook time:** 20 minutes| **Servings:** 2

Ingredients:
- 1-pound boneless chicken thighs
- ¼ cup white vinegar
- ½ cup water
- ¼ cup soy sauce
- ½ head garlic, peeled and smashed
- 2 bay leaves
- ½ teaspoon pepper
- 1 tsp oil

Directions:
1. Place all ingredients in the Ninja Foodi.
2. Install pressure lid. Close Ninja Foodi, press the pressure button, choose high settings, and set time to 10 minutes.
3. Once done cooking, do a quick release.
4. Open the lid and press the sauté button. Allow the sauce to reduce so that the chicken is fried slightly in its oil, around 10 minutes.
5. Serve and enjoy.

Nutrition: Calories 713, carbs 3.2g, protein 43.9g, fats 58.3g

Parsley Duck and Fennel

This Parsley Duck and Fennel recipe is perfectly cooked to bring out the sweet flavors and healthy nutrients in its ingredients. It can be served alongside favorite side dish.

Prep time: 10 minutes| **Cook time:** 25 minutes| **Servings:** 4

Ingredients:
- 2 duck breasts, boneless, skinless, halved
- 1 tablespoon olive oil
- 1 yellow onion, chopped
- 1 cup tomato sauce
- 2 fennel bulbs, shredded
- 2 teaspoons soy sauce
- Salt and black pepper to the taste

Directions:
1. Set the Foodi on Sauté mode, add the oil, heat it up, add the onion and sauté for 5 minutes.
2. Add the meat and the other ingredients, put the pressure lid on and cook on High for 20 minutes.
3. Release the pressure naturally for 10 minutes, divide everything between plates and serve.

Nutrition: calories 274, fat 14.4g, carbs 16.4g, protein 10.4g

Ginger-Balsamic Glazed Chicken

This is a common recipe that is loved by many because its taste is amazing! You need to make this delicious recipe and you will love it all the way!

Prep time: 10 minutes| **Cook time:** 15 minutes| **Servings:** 2

Ingredients:
- 4 chicken thighs, skinless
- ¼ cup balsamic vinegar
- 1 ½ tablespoons mustard

- 1 tablespoon ginger garlic paste
- 4 cloves of garlic, minced
- 1-inche fresh ginger root
- 2 tablespoons honey
- Salt and pepper to taste

Directions:

1. Place all ingredients in the Ninja Foodi. Stir to combine everything.

2. Install pressure lid. Close Ninja Foodi, press the manual button, choose high settings, and set time to 15 minutes.

3. Once done cooking, do a quick release. Remove pressure lid.

4. Mix and turnover chicken.

5. Cover, press roast, and roast for 5 minutes.

6. Serve and enjoy.

Nutrition: Calories 476; Carbs12.5g, Protein 32.4g, Fats 32.9g

Chapter 4: Beef, Pork and Lamb Recipes

Mustard Dredged Pork Chops

Prep time: 10 minutes| **Cook time:** 30 minutes |**Servings:** 4

Ingredients:

- 2 tablespoons butter
- 2 tablespoons Dijon mustard (Keto-Friendly)
- 4 pork chops
- Salt and pepper to taste
- 1 tablespoon fresh rosemary, coarsely chopped

Directions:

1. Take a bowl and add pork chops, cover with Dijon mustard and carefully sprinkle rosemary, salt and pepper
2. Let it marinate for 2 hours
3. Add butter and marinated pork chops to your Ninja Foodi pot
4. Lock lid and cook on Low-Medium Pressure for 30 minutes
5. Release pressure naturally over 10 minutes
6. Take the dish out, serve and enjoy!

Nutrition:

- Calories: 315
- Fat: 26g
- Carbohydrates: 1g
- Protein: 18g

Crazy Greek Lamb Gyros

Prep time: 10 minutes| **Cook time:** 25 minutes |**Servings:** 8

Ingredients:

- 8 garlic cloves
- 1 and ½ teaspoon salt
- 2 teaspoons dried oregano
- 1 and ½ cups water
- 2 pounds lamb meat, ground
- 2 teaspoons rosemary
- ½ teaspoon pepper
- 1 small onion, chopped
- 2 teaspoons ground marjoram

Directions:

1. Add onions, garlic, marjoram, rosemary, salt and pepper to a food processor
2. Process until combined well, add round lamb meat and process again
3. Press meat mixture gently into a loaf pan
4. Transfer the pan to your Ninja Foodi pot
5. Lock lid and select "Bake|Roast" mode
6. Bake for 25 minutes at 375 degrees F
7. Transfer to serving dish and enjoy!

Nutrition: Calories: 242, Fat: 15g, Carbohydrates: 2.4g, Protein: 21g

Healthy Cranberry Keto-Friendly BBQ Pork

Prep time: 10 minutes| **Cook time:** 45 minutes |**Servings:** 4

Ingredients:

- 3-4 pounds pork shoulder, boneless, fat trimmed

For Sauce

- 3 tablespoons liquid smoke
- 2 tablespoons tomato paste
- 2 cups fresh cranberries
- ¼ cup hot sauce (Keto-Friendly)
- 1|3 cup blackstrap molasses
- ½ cup water
- ½ cup apple cider vinegar
- 1 teaspoon salt
- 1 tablespoons adobo sauce (Keto Friendly and Sugar Free)

- 1 cup tomato puree (Keto-Friendly and Sugar Free)
- 1 chipotle pepper in adobo sauce, diced

Directions:

1. Cut pork against halves/thirds and keep it on the side
2. Set your Ninja Foodi to "SAUTE" mode and let it heat up
3. Add cranberries and water to the pot
4. Let them simmer for 4-5 minutes until cranberries start to pop, add rest of the sauce ingredients and simmer for 5 minutes more
5. Add pork to the pot and lock lid
6. Cook on HIGH pressure for 40 minutes
7. Quick release pressure
8. Use fork to shred the pork and serve on your favorite greens

Nutrition: Calories: 250, Fat: 17g, Carbohydrates: 5g, Protein: 15g

Mesmerizing Beef Sirloin Steak

Prep time: 5 minutes| **Cook time:** 17 minutes |**Servings:** 4

Ingredients:

- 3 tablespoons butter
- ½ teaspoon garlic powder
- 1-2 pounds beef sirloin steaks
- Salt and pepper to taste
- 1 garlic clove, minced

Directions:

1. Set your Ninja Foodi to sauté mode and add butter, let the butter melt
2. Add beef sirloin steaks
3. Saute for 2 minutes on each side
4. Add garlic powder, garlic clove, salt and pepper
5. Lock lid and cook on Medium-HIGH pressure for 15 minutes
6. Release pressure naturally over 10 minutes

7. Transfer prepare Steaks to serving platter, enjoy!

Nutrition: Calories: 246, Fat: 13g, Carbohydrates: 2g, Protein: 31g

Epic Beef Sausage Soup

Prep time: 10 minutes| Cook time: 30 minutes |**Servings:** 6

Ingredients:

- 1 tablespoon extra virgin olive oil
- 6 cups beef broth
- 1 pound organic beef sausage, cooked and sliced
- 2 cups sauerkraut
- 2 celery stalks, chopped
- 1 sweet onion, chopped
- 2 teaspoons garlic, minced
- 2 tablespoons butter
- 1 tablespoon hot mustard
- ½ teaspoon caraway seeds
- ½ cup sour cream
- 2 tablespoons fresh parsley, chopped

Directions:

1. Grease the inner pot of your Ninja Foodi with olive oil
2. Add broth, sausage, sauerkraut, celery, onion, garlic, butter, mustard, caraway seeds in the pot
3. Lock lid and cook on HIGH pressure for 30 minutes
4. Quick release pressure
5. Remove lid and stir in sour cream
6. Serve with a topping of parsley
7. Enjoy!

Nutrition: Calories: 165, Fat: 4g, Carbohydrates: 14g, Protein: 11g

Mesmerizing Pork Carnitas

Prep time: 10 minutes | **Cook time:** 25 minutes | **Servings:** 4

Ingredients:

- 2 pounds pork butt, chopped into 2 inch pieces
- 1 teaspoon salt
- ½ teaspoon oregano
- ½ teaspoon cumin
- 1 yellow onion, cut into half
- 6 garlic cloves, peeled and crushed
- ½ cup chicken broth

Directions:

1. Insert a pan into your Ninja Foodi and add pork
2. Season with salt, cumin, oregano and mix well, making sure that the pork is well seasoned
3. Take the orange and squeeze the orange juice all over
4. Add squeezed orange to into the insert pan as well
5. Add garlic cloves and onions
6. Pour ½ cup chicken broth into the pan
7. Lock the lid of the Ninja Foodi, making sure that the valve is sealed well
8. Set pressure to HIGH and let it cook for 20 minutes
9. Once the timer beeps, quick release the pressure
10. Open the lid and take out orange, garlic cloves, and onions
11. Set your Nina Foodi to Sauté mode and adjust the temperature to medium-high
12. Let the liquid simmer for 10-15 minutes
13. After most of the liquid has been reduced, press stop button
14. Close the Ninja Foodi with "Air Crisp" lid
15. Pressure broil option and set timer to 8 minutes
16. Take the meat and put it in wraps
17. Garnish with cilantro and enjoy!

Nutrition: Calories: 355, Fat: 13g, Carbohydrates: 9g, Protein: 43g

Authentic Beginner Friendly Pork Belly

Prep time: 10 minutes | **Cook time:** 40 minutes | **Servings:** 4

Ingredients:

- 1 pound pork belly
- ½-1 cup white wine vinegar
- 1 garlic clove
- 1 tablespoon olive oil
- Salt and pepper to taste

Directions:

1. Set your Ninja Foodi to "SAUTE" mode and add oil, let it heat up
2. Add pork and sear for 2-3 minutes until both sides are golden and crispy
3. Add vinegar until about a quarter inch, season with salt, pepper and garlic
4. Add garlic clove and Saute until the liquid comes to a boil
5. Lock lid and cook on HIGH pressure for 40 minutes
6. Once done, quick release pressure
7. Slice the meat and serve with the sauce
8. Enjoy!

Nutrition: Calories: 331, Fat: 21g, Carbohydrates: 2g, Protein: 19g

The Indian Beef Delight

Prep time: 15 minutes | **Cook time:** 20 minutes | **Servings:** 4

Ingredients:

- ½ yellow onion, chopped
- 1 tablespoon olive oil

- 2 garlic cloves, minced
- 1 jalapeno pepper, chopped
- 1 cup cherry tomatoes, quartered
- 1 teaspoon fresh lemon juice
- 1-2 pounds grass fed ground beef
- 1-2 pounds fresh collard greens, trimmed and chopped

Spices

- 1 teaspoon cumin, ground
- ½ teaspoon ginger, ground
- 1 teaspoon coriander, ground
- ½ teaspoon fennel seeds, ground
- ½ teaspoon cinnamon, ground
- Salt and pepper to taste
- ½ teaspoon turmeric, ground

Directions:

1. Set your Ninja Foodi to sauté mode and add garlic, onions
2. sauté for 3 minutes
3. Add jalapeno pepper, beef and spices
4. Lock lid and cook on Medium-HIGH pressure for 15 minutes
5. Release pressure naturally over 10 minutes, open lid
6. Add tomatoes, collard greens and sauté for 3 minutes
7. Stir in lemon juice, salt and pepper
8. Stir well
9. Once the dish is ready, transfer the dish to your serving bowl and enjoy!

Nutrition: Calories: 409, Fat: 16g, Carbohydrates: 5g, Protein: 56g

Warm and Beefy Meat Loaf

Prep time: 10 minutes| **Cook time:** 1 hour 10 minutes |**Servings:** 6

Ingredients:

- ½ cup onion, chopped
- 2 garlic cloves, minced
- ¼ cup sugar free ketchup
- 1 pound grass fed-lean ground beef
- ½ cup green bell pepper, seeded and chopped
- 1 cup cheddar cheese, grated
- 2 organic eggs, beaten
- 1 teaspoon dried thyme, crushed
- 3 cups fresh spinach, chopped
- 6 cups mozzarella cheese, freshly grated
- Black pepper to taste

Directions:

1. Take a bowl and add all of the listed ingredients except cheese and spinach
2. Place a wax paper on a smooth surface and arrange the meat over it
3. Top with spinach, cheese and roll the paper around the paper to form a nice meat loaf
4. Remove wax paper and transfer loaf to your Ninja Foodi
5. Lock lid and select "Bake|Roast" mode, setting the timer to 70 minutes and temperature to 380 degrees F
6. Let it bake and take the dish out once done
7. Serve and enjoy!

Nutrition: Calories: 409, Fat: 16g, Carbohydrates: 5g, Protein: 56g

The Ultimate One-Pot Beef Roast

Prep time: 10 minutes| **Cook time:** 40 minutes |**Servings:** 4

Ingredients:

- 2-3 pounds beef, chuck roast
- 4 carrots, chopped
- 3 garlic cloves,
- 2 tablespoons olive oil
- 2 tablespoons Italian seasoning
- 2 stalks celery, chopped
- 1 onion, chopped

- 1 cup beef broth
- 1 cup dry red wine

Directions:

1. Set your Ninja Foodi to "Saute" mode and add oil, let it heat up
2. Add roast beef to the pot and cook each side for 1-2 minute until browned
3. Transfer browned beef to plate
4. Add celery, carrot to the pot and top with garlic and onion
5. Add beef broth and wine to the pot, put roast on top of vegies
6. Spread seasoning on top and lock lid, Cook on HIGH pressure for 35 minutes
7. Release pressure naturally over 10 minutes
8. Serve and enjoy!

Nutrition: Calories: 299, Fat: 21g, Carbohydrates: 3g, Protein: 14g

Deliciously Spicy Pork Salad Bowl

Prep time: 10 minutes| **Cook time:** 90 minutes |**Servings:** 6

Ingredients:

- 4 pounds pork shoulder
- Butter as needed
- 2 teaspoons salt
- 2 cups chicken stock
- 1 teaspoon smoked paprika powder
- 1 teaspoon garlic powder
- 1 teaspoon black pepper
- 1 pinch dried oregano leaves
- 4 tablespoons coconut oil
- 6 garlic cloves

Directions:

1. Remove rind from pork and cut meat from bone, slice into large chunks
2. Trim fat off met
3. Set your Foodi to Saute mode and add oil, let it heat up
4. Once the oil is hot, layer chunks of meat in the bottom of the pot and Saute for around 30 minutes until browned
5. While the meat are being browned, peel garlic cloves and cut into small chunks
6. Once the meat is browned, transfer it to a large sized bowl
7. Add a few tablespoons of chicken stock to the pot an deglaze it, scraping off browned bits
8. Transfer browned bits to the bowl with meat chunks
9. Repeat if any more meat are left
10. Once done, add garlic, oregano leaves, smoked paprika, Garlic powder, pepper and salt to the meat owl and mix it up
11. Add all chicken stock to pot and bring to a simmer over Saute mode
12. Once done, return seasoned meat to the pot and lock lid, cook on HIGH pressure for 45 minutes. Release pressure naturally over 10 minutes
13. Open lid and shred the meat using fork, transfer shredded meat to a bowl and pour cooking liquid through a mesh to separate fat into the bowl with shredded meat
14. Serve with lime and enjoy!

Nutrition: Calories: 307, Fat: 23g, Carbohydrates: 8g, Protein: 15g

Decisive Kalua Pork

Prep time: 10 minutes| **Cook time:** 90 minutes |**Servings:** 4

Ingredients

- 4 pounds pork shoulder, cut into half
- ½ cup water
- 2 tablespoons olive oil
- Salt and pepper to taste
- 1 tablespoon liquid smoke
- Steamer green beans for serving (optional)

Directions:

1. Set your Ninja Foodi to "SAUTE" mode and add oil, let it heat up
2. Add pork, salt and pepper, brown each side for 3 minutes until both sides are slightly browned
3. Transfer them to a plate
4. Add water, liquid smoke to the pot and return the meat, stir
5. Lock lid and cook on HIGH pressure for 90 minutes, release pressure naturally over 10 minutes
6. Transfer meat to cutting board and shred using 2 forks, divide between serving plates and serve with the cooking liquid on top, add green beans on the side if you prefer
7. Enjoy!

Nutrition: Calories: 357, Fat: 28g, Carbohydrates: 2g, Protein: 20g

Perfect Sichuan Pork Soup

Prep time: 10 minutes| **Cook time:** 20 minutes |**Servings:** 6

Ingredients:

- 2 tablespoons olive oil
- 1 tablespoon garlic, minced
- 1 tablespoon fresh ginger, minced
- 2 tablespoons coconut aminos
- 2 tablespoons black vinegar
- 1-2 teaspoons stevia
- 1-2 teaspoons salt
- ½ onion, sliced
- 1 pound pork shoulder, cut into 2 inch chunks
- 2 pepper corns, crushed
- 3 cups water
- 3-4 cups bok choy, chopped
- ¼ cup fresh cilantro, chopped

Directions:

1. Pre-heat your Ninja Foodi by setting it to Saute mode on HIGH settings
2. Once the inner pot it hot enough, add oil and let heat until shimmering
3. Add garlic and ginger and Saute for 1-2 minutes
4. Add coconut aminos, vinegar, sweetener, pepper corn, salt, onion, pork, water and stir
5. Lock lid and cook on HIGH pressure for 20 minutes
6. Release pressure naturally over 10 minutes
7. Open lid and add bok choy, close lid and let it cook in the remaining heat for 10 minutes
8. Ladle soup into serving bowl and serve with topping of cilantro
9. Enjoy!

Nutrition: Calories: 256, Fat: 20g, Carbohydrates: 5g, Protein: 14g

Special "Swiss" Pork chops

Prep time: 5 minutes| **Cook time:** 18 minutes |**Servings:** 4

Ingredients:

- ½ cup Swiss cheese, shredded
- 4 pork chops, bone-in
- 6 bacon strips, cut in half
- Salt and pepper to taste
- 1 tablespoon butter

Directions:

1. Season pork chops with salt and pepper
2. Set your Foodi to sauté mode and add butter, let the butter heat up
3. Add pork chops and sauté for 3 minutes on each side
4. Add bacon strips and Swiss cheese
5. Lock lid and cook on Medium-LOW pressure for 15 minutes
6. Release pressure naturally over 10 minutes

7. Transfer steaks to serving platter, serve and enjoy!

Nutrition: Calories: 483, Fat: 40g, Carbohydrates: 0.7g, Protein: 27g

Fresh Korean Braised Ribs

Prep time: 10 minutes| **Cook time:** 45 minutes |**Servings:** 6

Ingredients:

- 1 teaspoon olive oil
- 2 green onions, cut into 1 inch length
- 3 garlic cloves, smashed
- 3 quarter sized ginger slices
- 4 pounds beef short ribs, 3 inches thick, cut into 3 rib portions
- ½ cup water
- ½ cup coconut aminos
- ¼ cup dry white wine
- 2 teaspoons sesame oil
- Mince green onions for serving

Directions:

1. Set your Ninja Foodi to "SAUTE" mode and add oil, let it shimmer

2. Add green onions, garlic, ginger, Saute for 1 minute

3. Add short ribs, water, aminos, wine, sesame oil and stir until the ribs are coated well

4. Lock lid and cook on HIGH pressure for 45 minutes

5. Release pressure naturally over 10 minutes

6. Remove short ribs from pot and serve with the cooking liquid

7. Enjoy!

Nutrition: Calories: 423, Fat: 35g, Carbohydrates: 4g, Protein: 22g

Wise Corned Beef

Prep time: 10 minutes| **Cook time:** 60 minutes |**Servings:** 4

Ingredients:

- 4 pounds beef brisket
- 2 garlic cloves, peeled and minced
- 2 yellow onions, peeled and sliced
- 11 ounces celery, thinly sliced
- 1 tablespoon dried dill
- 3 bay leaves
- 4 cinnamon sticks, cut into halves
- Salt and pepper to taste
- 17 ounces water

Directions:

1. Take a bowl and add beef, add water and cover, let it soak for 2-3 hours

2. Drain and transfer to the Ninja Foodi

3. Add celery, onions, garlic, bay leaves, dill, cinnamon, dill, salt, pepper and rest of the water to the Ninja Foodi

4. Stir and combine it well

5. Lock lid and cook on HIGH pressure for 50 minutes

6. Release pressure naturally over 10 minutes

7. Transfer meat to cutting board and slice, divide amongst plates and pour the cooking liquid (alongside veggies) over the servings

8. Enjoy!

Nutrition: Calories: 289, Fat: 21g, Carbohydrates: 14g, Protein: 9g

Easy-Going Kid Friendly Pork Chops

Prep time: 15 minutes| **Cook time:** 5-10 minutes |**Servings:** 4

Ingredients:

- 3-4 pork chops -12 to ¾ inch thick each
- 1 egg, beaten
- 1-2 cups Almond flour as needed
- Salt and pepper to taste
- 1-2 cups almond meal
- ½ cup onions, chopped

- 2-4 garlic cloves, squashed and chopped
- 1 tablespoons butter
- 1-2 tablespoons coconut oil

Directions:

1. Set your Ninja Foodi to "Saute" mode and add butter, let it heat up
2. Dredge the pork chops in beaten egg, then in flour and finally in almond meal
3. Add them to the pot and brown all sides
4. Add onions and cook for a minute
5. Add garlic and cook for 1 minute more
6. Transfer the browned meat, onion and garlic to a plate, make sure to keep the drippings in the pot
7. Add 2-3 tablespoons of water and place and place a steamer rack in your pot
8. Add browned pork chops on the steamer and lock lid
9. Cook on HIGH Pressure for 5 minutes, once done, let the pressure release naturally over 10 minutes
10. Remove from pot and serve
11. Enjoy!

Nutrition: Calories: 446, Fat: 25g, Carbohydrates: 6g, Protein: 21g

The Classical Corned Beef and Cabbage

Prep time: 15 minutes| **Cook time:** 90 minutes |**Servings:** 4

Ingredients:

- 3 pounds cabbage, cut into eight wedges
- 1 onion, quartered
- 1 celery stalk, quartered
- 1 corned beef spice packet
- 4 cups water
- 1 pound carrots, peeled and cut to 2 and ½ inch length

Directions:

1. Rinse beef thoroughly and add to Ninja Foodi
2. Add onion and celery to the pot
3. Add water and lock lid
4. Cook on HIGH pressure for 90 minutes, quick release pressure
5. Transfer beef to a plate
6. Add carrots, and cabbage to the pot, lock lid again and cook on HIGH pressure for 5 minutes more
7. Quick release pressure
8. Transfer veggies to the plate with corned beef
9. Pass the gravy through a gravy strainer over the beef and serve
10. Enjoy!

Nutrition: Calories: 531, Fat: 45g, Carbohydrates: 9g, Protein: 25g

Elegant Beef Curry

Prep time: 10 minutes| **Cook time:** 20 minutes |**Servings:** 4

Ingredients:

- 2 pounds beef steak, cubed
- 2 tablespoons extra virgin olive oil
- 1 tablespoon Dijon mustard
- 2 and ½ tablespoons curry powder
- 2 yellow onions, peeled and chopped
- 2 garlic cloves, peeled and minced
- 10 ounces canned coconut milk
- 2 tablespoons tomato sauce
- Salt and pepper to taste

Directions:

1. Set your Ninja Foodi to "Saute" mode and add oil, let it heat up
2. Add onions, garlic, stir cook for 4 minutes
3. Add mustard, stir and cook for 1 minute
4. Add beef and stir until all sides are browned

5. Add curry powder, salt and pepper, stir cook for 2 minutes

6. Add coconut milk and tomato sauce, stir and cove

7. Lock lid and cook on HIGH pressure for 10 minutes

8. Release pressure naturally over 10 minutes

9. Serve and enjoy!

Nutrition: Calories: 275, Fat: 12g, Carbohydrates: 12g, Protein: 27g

Chapter 5: Fish and Seafood Recipes

Mackerel and Zucchini Patties

Prep time: 10 minutes| **Cook time:** 15 minutes| **Servings:** 6

Ingredients:

- 10 ounces mackerel
- 1 medium zucchini
- ½ cup coconut flour
- 2 eggs
- 1 teaspoon baking soda
- 1 tablespoon lemon juice
- 1 teaspoon oregano
- 1 tablespoon olive oil
- 2 garlic cloves
- 1 teaspoon red chili flakes

Directions:

Minced the mackerel and place it in a mixing bowl. Wash the zucchini carefully and grate it. Add the grated zucchini in the minced fish. Sprinkle the mixture with the baking soda, lemon juice, oregano, and chile flakes. Peel the garlic cloves and slice them. Add the garlic to the fish mixture. Whisk the eggs in the separate bowl. Add the whisked eggs to the fish mixture. Sprinkle the mixture with the coconut flour and knead the dough until smooth. Spray the pressure cooker with the olive oil. Set the pressure cooker to "Sauté" mode. Make medium-sized patties and put them into the pressure cooker. Sauté the dish for 5 minutes. Flip the patties to cook on the other side. Sauté the dish for 10 minutes. When the cooking time ends, open the pressure cooker lid and remove the cooked patties. Let the dish rest. Let the dish rest briefly and serve.

Nutrition: calories 213, fat 13.7, fiber 3.8, carbs 7.1, protein 15

Shrimp and Tomato Delight

Prep time: 10 minutes| **Cook time:** 5 minutes| **Servings:** 4

Ingredients:

- 3 tablespoons unsalted butter
- 1 tablespoon garlic
- ½ teaspoon red pepper flakes
- 1 and ½ cup onion, chopped
- 1 can (14 and ½ ounces) tomatoes, diced
- 1 teaspoon dried oregano
- 1 teaspoon salt
- 1 pound frozen shrimp, peeled
- 1 cup crumbled feta cheese
- ½ cup black olives, sliced
- ½ cup parsley, chopped

Directions:

1. Pre-heat your Ninja Foodi by setting in in the Saute mode on HIGH settings, add butter and let it melt. Add garlic, pepper flakes, cook for 1 minute
2. Add onion, tomato, oregano, salt and stir well. Add frozen shrimp
3. Lock lid and cook on HIGH pressure for 1 minute. Quick release pressure
4. Mix shrimp with tomato broth, let it cool and serve with a sprinkle of feta, olives, and parsley
5. Enjoy!

Fish Pie

Prep time: 15 minutes| **Cook time:** 30 minutes| **Servings:** 8

Ingredients:

- 1 tablespoon curry paste
- 1 teaspoon curry
- 1 cup cream
- 1 pound salmon fillet
- ¼ cup garlic clove
- ½ tablespoon salt

- 1 teaspoon cilantro
- 1 teaspoon olive oil
- ¼ cup of fish sauce
- 1 onion
- 1 teaspoon red chili flakes
- 1 tablespoon fresh ginger
- 10 ounces keto dough

Directions:

Roll the keto dough using a rolling pin. Spray the pressure cooker with the olive oil. Place the rolled dough into the pressure cooker. Combine the curry paste, curry, cream, salt, cilantro, fish sauce, water, chili flakes, and fresh ginger in a mixing bowl and blend well and stir well. Chop the salmon fillet and put it in the mixing bowl. Add curry paste mixture and mix well. Put the fish mixture in the middle of the pie crust. Grate the fresh ginger and sprinkle the top of the pie. Peel the onion, slice it, and add it to the top of the fish pie and close the lid. Set the pressure cooker to "Pressure" mode. Cook the dish on for 30 minutes. When the pie is cooked, remove it from the pressure cooker and slice it. Serve the pie warm.

Nutrition: calories 256, fat 8.5, fiber 5.3, carbs 13, protein 32.8

Paprika Salmon

Prep time: 15 minutes| Servings: 2

Ingredients:

- 2 salmon fillets
- 2 teaspoons avocado oil
- 2 teaspoons paprika
- Salt and pepper to taste

Directions:

1. Coat the salmon with oil. Season with salt, pepper and paprika.
2. Place in the Ninja Foodi basket. Set it to air crisp function.
3. Seal the crisping lid. Cook at 390 degrees for 7 minutes.

Serving Suggestion: Garnish with lemon slices.
Tip: Cooking depends on the fish fillet thickness. You may need to cook longer for thicker cuts.
Nutrition: Calories 248, Total Fat 11.9g, Cholesterol 78mg, Sodium 79mg, Total Carbohydrate 1.5g, Dietary Fiber 1g, Total Sugars 0.2g, Protein 34.9g, Potassium 748mg

Cool Shrimp Zoodles

Prep time: 5 minutes| **Cook time:** 3 minutes | **Servings:** 4

Ingredients:

- 4 cups zoodles
- 1 tablespoon basil, chopped
- 2 tablespoons Ghee
- 1 cup vegetable stock
- 2 garlic cloves, minced
- 2 tablespoons olive oil
- ½ lemon
- ½ teaspoon paprika

Directions:

1. Set your Ninja Foodi to Saute mode and add ghee, let it heat up
2. Add olive oil as well. Add garlic and cook for 1 minute
3. Add lemon juice, shrimp and cook for 1 minute
4. Stir in rest of the ingredients and lock lid, cook on LOW pressure for 5 minutes
5. Quick release pressure and serve . Enjoy!

Calamari in Tomato Sauce

Prep time: 10 minutes| **Cook time:** 13 minutes| **Servings:** 4

Ingredients:

- 12 ounces calamari
- 1 white onion
- 1 teaspoon cilantro
- 3 garlic cloves

- 1 teaspoon ground ginger
- ¼ cup fish stock
- 1 teaspoon fresh thyme
- ¼ cup wine
- ¼ cup of water
- 1 tablespoon olive oil
- 3 medium tomatoes
- ½ teaspoon ground white pepper
- 1 teaspoon lime juice

Directions:

Wash the calamari carefully and peel it. Slice the calamari into medium-thick slices. Slice the garlic cloves, dice the onion, and c. hop the fresh thyme and tomatoes. Set the pressure cooker to "Sauté" mode. Put the sliced calamari into the pressure cooker and sprinkle it with the olive oil. Sauté the dish for 5 minutes. Add the garlic, onion, thyme, and tomatoes to the pressure cooker. Sprinkle the dish with the water, wine, ground ginger, lime juice, and fish stock, stir well, and close the lid. Set the pressure cooker to "Sauté" mode. Stew the dish for 8 minutes. Remove the cooked calamari from the pressure cooker. Serve the dish hot.

Nutrition: calories 238, fat 6.1, fiber 2, carbs 16.64, protein 29

Stuffed Snapper with Onions

Prep time: 10 minutes| **Cook time:** 20 minutes| **Servings:** 4

Ingredients:

- 1 pound snapper
- 2 white onions
- ½ cup dill
- 1 tablespoon olive oil
- 3 garlic cloves
- 1 teaspoon Erythritol
- ½ tablespoon of sea salt
- 1 teaspoon turmeric
- 1 teaspoon oregano
- ½ teaspoon cumin
- 1 teaspoon ground coriander
- 1 teaspoon dried celery root
- 4 ounces mushrooms

Directions:

Peel the snapper and cut it crosswise. Sprinkle the fish with sea salt. Peel the onions and dice them. Peel the garlic cloves and slice them. Pour the olive oil into the pressure cooker and preheat it on the "Sauté" mode. Add the diced onions and sliced garlic. Stir the mixture and cook it for 4 minutes and mix well. Remove the cooked onion mixture from the pressure cooker and chill it well. Chop the dill and sprinkle the cooked onion mixture with it. Add Erythritol, turmeric, oregano, cumin, ground coriander, and celery root. Dice the mushrooms. Add the mushrooms to the onion mixture. Fill the snapper with the onion mixture and wrap the fish in aluminum foil. Place the wrapped fish on the trivet and put it into the pressure cooker. Cook the dish on the "Steam" mode for 20 minutes. When the dish is cooked, open the pressure cooker lid and remove the fish. Discard the aluminum foil and chop the fish, if desired, before serving.

Nutrition: calories 230, fat 6.1, fiber 2.7, carbs 12, protein 32.7

Cod Chowder

Prep time: 10 minutes| **Cook time:** 35 minutes| **Servings:** 8

Ingredients:

- 2 tablespoons fresh marjoram
- 1 teaspoon salt
- 3 cups of water
- 1 cup cream
- 1 onion
- 7 ounces eggplant
- 1 carrot
- 7 ounces cod

mixture. Sprinkle the salad with the olive oil and stir it carefully using a so as not to damage the fish. Serve immediately.

Nutrition: calories 123, fat 6.5, fiber 1, carbs 5.29, protein 11

Tasty Cuttlefish

Prep time: 20 minutes| **Cook time:** 13 minutes| **Servings:** 6

Ingredients:

- 1 pound squid
- 1 tablespoon minced garlic
- 1 teaspoon onion powder
- 1 tablespoon lemon juice
- 1 tablespoon chives
- 1 teaspoon salt
- 1 teaspoon white pepper
- 3 tablespoons fish sauce
- 2 tablespoons butter
- ¼ chile pepper

Directions:

Slice the squid. Combine the minced garlic, onion powder, chives, salt, and white pepper together in a mixing bowl and stir well and stir. Chop the chile pepper and add it to the spice mixture. Combine the sliced squid and spice mixture together, stirring well. Sprinkle the seafood mixture with the lemon juice and fish sauce and stir. Let the mixture rest for 10 minutes. Set the pressure cooker to "Sauté" mode. Add the butter into the pressure cooker and melt it. Place the sliced squid mixture into the pressure cooker and close the lid. Cook the dish for 13 minutes. When the dish is cooked, remove the food from the pressure cooker. Sprinkle the dish with the liquid from the cooked squid and serve.

Nutrition: calories 112, fat 4.9, fiber 0, carbs 3.92, protein 12

Spicy Whitebait

Prep time: 10 minutes| **Cook time:** 10 minutes| **Servings:** 3

Ingredients:

- 1 teaspoon red chile flakes
- 1 tablespoon sour cream
- 4 tablespoons garlic sauce
- 1 pound whitebait
- 3 tablespoons butter
- ½ teaspoon sage
- 1 teaspoon oregano
- 1 teaspoon olive oil
- ½ cup almond flour
- ¼ cup milk
- 1 egg
- ½ teaspoon ground ginger

Directions:

Make fillets from the whitebait. Combine the chile flakes, sage, oregano, and ground ginger in a bowl and mix well and stir. Rub the whitebait fillets with the spice mixture. Let the fish rest for 5 minutes. Meanwhile, beat the egg in a separate bowl and whisk it. Add the milk and flour and stir until smooth. Add the sour cream and stir. Dip the whitebait fillets in the egg mixture. Set the pressure cooker to "Pressure" mode. Add the butter into the pressure cooker and melt it. Add the whitebait fillets and close the pressure cooker. Cook the dish on for 10 minutes. When the cooking time ends, release the remaining pressure and open the pressure cooker lid. Transfer the whitebait in a serving plate.

Nutrition: calories 472, fat 29.8, fiber 3.1, carbs 7.4, protein 43.2

- 1 teaspoon ground black pepper
- 1 teaspoon butter
- 3 tablespoons chives
- ½ teaspoon nutmeg
- ½ cup dill
- 2 ounces fresh ginger

Directions:

Combine the water, cream, butter, and ground black pepper in a bowl and mix well and stir. Pour the cream mixture into the pressure cooker. Sprinkle the mixture with the salt, chives, nutmeg, and fresh ginger. Peel the onion, eggplants, and carrot. Grate the carrot and put it into the pressure cooker. Dice the onion and chop the eggplant. Set the pressure cooker to "Sauté" mode. Add the cod and the vegetables to the pressure cooker. Sprinkle the mixture with the fresh marjoram. Chop the dill. Close the pressure cooker lid and cook the dish on for 35 minutes. When the cooking time ends, release the remaining pressure and open the pressure cooker lid. Ladle the chowder into serving bowls and sprinkle the bowls with the chopped dill. Serve the chowder hot.

Nutrition: calories 99, fat 3.1, fiber 3, carbs 11.7, protein 7.7

Awesome Sock-Eye Salmon

Prep time: 5 minutes| **Cook time:** 5 minutes| **Servings:** 4

Ingredients:

- 4 sockeye salmon fillets
- 1 teaspoon Dijon mustard
- 1/4 teaspoon garlic, minced
- 1/4 teaspoon onion powder
- 1/4 teaspoon lemon pepper
- 1/2 teaspoon garlic powder
- 1/4 teaspoon salt
- 2 tablespoons olive oil
- 1 and 1/2 cup of water

Directions:

1. Take a bowl and add mustard, lemon juice, onion powder, lemon pepper, garlic powder, salt, olive oil. Brush spice mix over salmon
2. Add water to Instant Pot. Place rack and place salmon fillets on rack
3. Lock lid and cook on LOW pressure for 7 minutes
4. Quick release pressure. Serve and enjoy!

Nutrition: Calories: 353, Fat: 25g, Carbohydrates: 0.6g, Protein: 40g

Mackerel Salad

Prep time: 10 minutes| **Cook time:** 10 minutes| **Servings:** 6

Ingredients:

- 1 cup lettuce
- 8 ounces mackerel
- 1 teaspoon salt
- 1 teaspoon paprika
- 1 tablespoon olive oil
- ½ teaspoon rosemary
- 1 garlic clove
- ½ cup fish stock
- 1 teaspoon oregano
- 7 ounces tomatoes
- 1 large cucumber
- 1 red onion

Directions:

Wash the lettuce and chop it. Rub the mackerel with the salt, paprika, and rosemary. Set the pressure cooker to "Pressure" mode. Place the spiced mackerel into the pressure cooker. Add the fish stock and close the lid. Cook the dish for 10 minutes. Peel the garlic clove and slice Peel the red onion and slice it. Combine the sliced onion with the chopped lettuce. Slice cucumber and chop tomatoes. Add the vegetables to the lettuce mixture. When the mackerel is cooked, remove it from the pre cooker and let it rest briefly. Chop the fish roughly. Add the chopped fish in the lettu

Monkfish Stew

Prep time: 10 minutes| **Cook time:** 30 minutes| **Servings:** 7

Ingredients:

- 1 pound monkfish fillet
- ½ cup white wine
- 1 teaspoon salt
- 1 teaspoon white pepper
- 1 medium carrot
- 2 white onions
- 1 cup fish stock
- 3 tablespoons fish sauce
- 1 tablespoon olive oil
- 1 teaspoon oregano
- ½ teaspoon fresh rosemary
- 1 cup of water
- 1 teaspoon sugar
- 1 teaspoon thyme
- 1 teaspoon coriander

Directions:

Chop the monkfish fillet roughly and sprinkle it with the salt, white pepper, fish sauce, oregano, fresh oregano, sugar, thyme, and coriander and stir well. Let the fish rest for 5 minutes. Peel the onions and carrot and chop the vegetables. Set the pressure cooker to "Sauté" mode. Put the chopped vegetables and monkfish into the pressure cooker. Sprinkle the mixture with the white wine, water, and olive oil. Mix well and close the pressure cooker lid. Cook the dish on for 30 minutes. When the stew is cooked, open the pressure cooker lid and let the stew rest for 10 minutes. Transfer the stew to a serving bowl and serve.

Nutrition: calories 251, fat 14, fiber 5, carbs 15, protein 17

Seafood Paella

Prep time: 10 minutes| **Cook time:** 15 minutes| **Servings:** 5

Ingredients:

- 1 cup cauliflower rice
- 8 ounces shrimp
- 5 ounces mussels
- 2 cups fish stock
- 1 cup of water
- 1 tablespoon of sea salt
- 1 small chile pepper
- 1 teaspoon curry
- 1 teaspoon turmeric
- 1 tablespoon oregano
- 1 tablespoon fish sauce
- 1 teaspoon paprika
- 3 garlic cloves
- 1 tablespoon butter

Directions:

Peel the shrimp and combine them with the mussels. Place the seafood into the pressure cooker. Add cauliflower rice, salt, curry, turmeric, oregano, and paprika and stir well. Combine the fish stock, fish sauce, and butter together in a mixing bowl and blend well. Pour water mixture into the pressure cooker. Peel the garlic and slice it. Chop the chile pepper. Sprinkle the cauliflower rice mixture with the sliced garlic and chopped chile pepper. Stir briefly using a wooden spoon. Close the pressure cooker lid and set the pressure cooker mode to "Steam". Cook for 15 minutes. When the dish is cooked, remove the food from the pressure cooker. Transfer the paella to a serving bowl.

Nutrition: calories 130, fat 4.7, fiber 1.3, carbs 4.9, protein 16.8

Fish Curry

Prep time: 10 minutes| **Cook time:** 10 minutes| **Servings:** 5

Ingredients:

- 1 tablespoon curry paste
- 1 teaspoon curry
- 1 cup cream
- 1 pound salmon fillet
- ¼ cup garlic clove
- ½ tablespoon salt
- 1 teaspoon cilantro
- ¼ cup of fish sauce
- ½ cup of water
- 1 onion
- 1 teaspoon red chile flakes
- 1 tablespoon fresh ginger

Directions:

Chop the salmon fillet roughly and transfer it to the pressure cooker. Combine the cream and fish sauce in a mixing bowl. Sprinkle the liquid mixture with the curry paste and curry and blend until smooth. Peel the garlic cloves and onion. Chop the vegetables and add them to the cream mixture. Grate the ginger and add the ginger, chili flakes, water, salt, and cilantro and mix well. Pour it onto the chopped salmon and coat the fish well. Add the curried fish to the pressure cooker. Close the lid and set the pressure cooker mode to "Pressure." Cook the dish for 10 minutes. When the cooking time ends, release the remaining pressure and open the lid. Transfer the dish to serving bowls.

Nutrition: calories 264, fat 16.2, fiber 2, carbs 7.99, protein 22

Red Chili Anchovy

Prep time: 15 minutes| **Cook time:** 8 minutes| **Servings:** 3

Ingredients:

- 1 red chile pepper
- 10 ounces anchovies
- 4 tablespoons butter
- 1 teaspoon of sea salt
- ½ teaspoon paprika
- 1 teaspoon red chile flakes
- 1 tablespoon basil
- 1 teaspoon dried dill
- 1 teaspoon rosemary
- ⅓ cup breadcrumbs

Directions:

Remove the seeds from the chile pepper and slice it. Combine the chile flakes, paprika, sea salt, basil, dry dill, and rosemary together in a shallow bowl and stir well. Sprinkle the anchovies with the spice mixture. Combine well using your hands. Add sliced chile pepper and Let the mixture rest for 10 minutes. Set the pressure cooker to "Sauté" mode. Add the butter into the pressure cooker and melt it. Dip the spiced anchovies in the breadcrumbs and put the fish in the melted butter. Cook the anchovies for 4 minutes on each side. When the fish is cooked, remove it from the pressure cooker and drain it on a paper towel to remove any excess oil. Serve immediately.

Nutrition: calories 356, fat 25, fiber 1, carbs 4.17, protein 28

Parsley Marinated Shrimps

Prep time: 20 minutes| **Cook time:** 7 minutes| **Servings:** 3

Ingredients:

- 2 tablespoons fresh cilantro
- 2 tablespoons apple cider vinegar
- 1 tablespoon lemon juice
- ½ teaspoon lemon zest
- ½ tablespoon salt
- ¼ cup white wine
- 1 teaspoon brown sugar
- ½ teaspoon ground ginger

- 1 tablespoon olive oil
- ½ tablespoon minced garlic
- 1 teaspoon nutmeg
- 1 cup of water
- .5½ pound shrimp
- 1 cup parsley

Directions:

Chop the cilantro and parsley. Combine the lemon juice, apple cider vinegar, lemon zest, salt, white wine, and sugar together in a mixing bowl. Stir the mixture until sugar and salt are dissolved. Peel the shrimp and devein and put them in the lemon juice mixture. Add the chopped cilantro and parsley and stir well. Add ground ginger, olive oil, nutmeg, and water. Mix up the shrimp mixture well and let it marinate for 15 minutes. Set the pressure cooker to "Pressure" mode. Transfer the marinated shrimp into the pressure cooker and cook the dish for 7 minutes. When the cooking time ends, release the remaining pressure and open the pressure cooker lid. Serve the shrimp warm or keep them in the marinated liquid in your refrigerator.

Nutrition: calories 143, fat 6, fiber 1, carbs 5.63, protein 16

Halibut with the Soy Ginger Sauce

Prep time: 10 minutes| **Cook time:** 9 minutes| **Servings:** 6

Ingredients:

- 1 pound halibut
- 1 tablespoon butter
- 3 tablespoons fish sauce
- 1 teaspoon rosemary
- 1 tablespoon cream
- 1 teaspoon ground white pepper
- ½ cup of soy sauce
- 2 tablespoons fresh ginger
- 1 teaspoon olive oil
- 1 teaspoon ground ginger

Directions:

Cut the halibut into the fillets and. Sprinkle the halibut with the rosemary and ground white pepper. Set the pressure cooker to "Sauté" mode. Add the butter into the pressure cooker and melt it at the sauté mode. Place the fish into the pressure cooker. Sauté the halibut fillets into the pressure cooker for 2 minutes on both sides. Combine the fish sauce, cream, soy sauce, fresh ginger, olive oil, and ground ginger together in the bowl and mix well. Sprinkle the halibut fillet with the ginger sauce and close the pressure cooker lid. Cook the dish on "Pressure" mode for 5 minutes. When the cooking time ends, open the pressure cooker lid and remove the halibut fillets from the pressure cooker vessel gently so not to damage the dish and let it rest before serving.

Nutrition: calories 240, fat 17.5, fiber 1, carbs 7.01, protein 13

Cod Stew

Prep time: 15 minutes| **Cook time:** 30 minutes| **Servings:** 8

Ingredients:

- 1 pound cod
- 1 large onion
- ¼ cup garlic cloves
- 3 red bell peppers
- 1 teaspoon cilantro
- 1 tablespoon oregano
- 1 teaspoon turmeric
- 4 cups chicken stock
- 1 cup black soybeans, canned
- 1 teaspoon of sea salt
- ¼ cup of fish sauce
- ½ cup of water
- 1 teaspoon red chile flakes
- 1 tablespoon fresh ginger

- ½ cup parsley
- 1 tablespoon ground black pepper
- 1 teaspoon white pepper

Directions:

Chop the cod roughly and add it to a mixing bowl. Peel the onion and garlic cloves and dice them and add to the cod. Combine the cilantro, turmeric, sea salt, chili flakes, ground black pepper, and white pepper together in a separate bowl and mix well and stir well. Add the spice mixture to the cod. Add the canned black soybeans and ginger. Chop the parsley. Transfer the cod mixture into the pressure cooker. Add the chicken stock, water, and fish sauce. Sprinkle the stew mixture with the chopped parsley. Stir the stew mixture using a wooden spoon and close the lid. Set the pressure cooker to "Sauté" mode. Cook the dish on for 30 minutes. When the stew is cooked, let it cool briefly and serve.

Nutrition: calories 203, fat 2.2, fiber 5, carbs 27.8, protein 19

Sriracha Shrimp

Prep time: 10 minutes| **Cook time:** 8 minutes| **Servings:** 6

Ingredients:

- 1 pound shrimp
- 3 tablespoons minced garlic
- 1 tablespoon sriracha
- 1 tablespoon sesame oil
- 1 teaspoon salt
- 1 teaspoon ground black pepper
- 1 teaspoon ground ginger
- ⅓ cup fish stock
- 1 tablespoon butter

Directions:

Peel the shrimp and combine them with the sriracha in a mixing bowl and stir well and sprinkle it with the sesame oil, minced garlic, salt, ground black pepper, ground ginger, and fish stock and stir well. Toss everything well. Place the sriracha shrimp into the pressure cooker. Set the pressure cooker to "Pressure" mode. Add the butter and close the pressure cooker lid. Cook the dish on for 8 minutes. When the dish is cooked, remove the food from the pressure cooker. Let the dish rest. Let the dish rest briefly and serve.

Nutrition: calories 125, fat 5.4, fiber 0, carbs 2.33, protein 16

Tuna and Shirataki Noodles Salad

Prep time: 10 minutes| **Cook time:** 12 minutes| **Servings:** 6

Ingredients:

- 5 ounces Shirataki noodles
- 1 pound tuna
- 1 tablespoon olive oil
- 1 teaspoon ground black pepper
- 3 tablespoons sour cream
- 1 teaspoon ground ginger
- 5 tablespoon fish stock
- 1 tablespoon soy sauce
- 6 ounces Parmesan cheese
- 1 cup black olives
- 1 cup hot water

Directions:

Combine the ground black pepper and ground ginger together in a bowl and mix well and stir. Chop the tuna and add it to the ground black pepper mixture, stirring well. Cut the cheese into the cubes. Set the pressure cooker to "Steam" mode. Place the chopped tuna into the pressure cooker and cook it for 12 minutes. Combine the sliced black olives, cheese cubes, olive oil in the mixing bowl. Add soy sauce and fish stock. Sprinkle the mixture with the sour cream. When the tuna is cooked, release the pressure and open the instant lid. Chill the chopped tuna. Combine hot water and noodles together and let them sit for 15 minutes. Rinse the noodles and place them in the black olive mixture. Add the chilled chopped tuna and toss the salad gently. Transfer the salad to serving bowls.

Nutrition: calories 301, fat 18.3, fiber 3.4, carbs 3.3, protein 30.2

Tomato Snapper

Prep time: 10 minutes| **Cook time:** 15 minutes| **Servings:** 4

Ingredients:

- ½ cup tomato juice
- 1 large onion
- ½ teaspoon salt
- 1 tablespoon basil
- 1 teaspoon oregano
- 4 garlic cloves
- 1 tablespoon butter
- ½ cup chicken stock
- 1 pound snapper
- 2 tablespoons fish sauce

Directions:

Remove the skin from the snapper, make small slits into the surface of the skin, and set aside. Peel the onion and slice it. Combine the salt, basil, oregano, and fish sauce together in a mixing bowl and stir well. Rub the peeled fish with the spice mixture. Peel the garlic cloves and slice them. Set the pressure cooker to "Pressure" mode. Fill the snapper with the sliced garlic and onion and place the fish into the pressure cooker. Add tomato juice and close the lid. Cook the dish on mode for 15 minutes. When the cooking time ends, remove the snapper from the pressure cooker carefully so as not to damage the fish. Sprinkle the fish with the tomato juice from the pressure cooker. Let it rest briefly and serve.

Nutrition: calories 204, fat 5.1, fiber 1.2, carbs 6.5, protein 31.2

Marjoram Salmon

Prep time: 10 minutes| **Cook time:** 15 minutes| **Servings:** 6

Ingredients:

- 1 pound salmon fillet
- 1 tablespoon marjoram
- ½ teaspoon rosemary
- 1 tablespoons salt
- ½ cup dill
- 1 cup of water
- 1 teaspoon cilantro
- 1 tablespoon paprika
- 1 teaspoon butter
- 1 teaspoon onion powder

Directions:

Combine the marjoram, rosemary, and salt in a small bowl. Rub the salmon fillet with the spice mixture. Chop the dill and combine it with the onion powder and paprika in a mixing bowl. Add cilantro and stir well. Place the salmon fillet on the steamer rack and transfer it to the pressure cooker. Set the pressure cooker to "Steam" mode. Sprinkle the salmon with the dill mixture. Close the pressure cooker and cook the fish for 15 minutes. When the cooking time ends, release the remaining pressure and let the salmon rest briefly. Transfer the dish to a serving plate.

Nutrition: calories 127, fat 6.2, fiber 1, carbs 1.17, protein 16

Crunchy Cod

Prep time: 10 minutes| **Cook time:** 10 minutes| **Servings:** 5

Ingredients:

- 12 ounces cod fillet
- 3 eggs
- 1 cup coconut flour
- ⅓ cup pork rinds

- 1 teaspoon salt
- 2 tablespoons olive oil
- 1 teaspoon ground white pepper
- 1 teaspoon ground ginger
- 1 tablespoon turmeric
- 2 teaspoons sesame seeds
- ¼ teaspoon red chili flakes

Directions:

Whisk the eggs in a mixing bowl using a hand mixer. Add the coconut flour and continue to mix the mixture until smooth. Sprinkle the cod fillets with the salt, ground ginger, ground white pepper, and chili flakes. Add turmeric and mix well. Dip the cod fillets in the egg mixture. Sprinkle the fish with the pork rinds and sesame seeds. Pour olive oil into the pressure cooker and preheat it on the "Sauté" mode. Add the cod fillets and cook them for 5 minutes on each side. When the cod fillets are cooked, remove them from the pressure cooker and transfer the dish to paper towel drain. Rest briefly before serving.

Nutrition: calories 198, fat 12, fiber 1.6, carbs 3.5, protein 19.9

Smoked Salmon Bars

Prep time: 15 minutes| **Cook time:** 25 minutes| **Servings:** 6

Ingredients:

- 9 ounces keto dough
- 1 tablespoon olive oil
- 1 teaspoon butter
- ½ teaspoon rosemary
- 1 teaspoon salt
- 9 ounces smoked salmon
- 6 ounces mozzarella cheese
- 1 teaspoon fresh thyme
- 1 tablespoon tomato paste
- 1 teaspoon garlic sauce

Directions:

Roll the dough using a rolling pin. Spread the pressure cooker vessel with the butter. Place the rolled dough into the pressure cooker. Sprinkle the dough with the olive oil and rosemary. Chop the smoked salmon and sprinkle it with the salt and mix well and stir. Slice the mozzarella cheese. Sprinkle the keto dough with the garlic sauce and tomato paste. Add the smoked salmon and sliced cheese. Sprinkle the dish with the fresh thyme and close the lid. Cook the dish on the "Sauté" mode for 25 minutes. When the cooking time ends, open the pressure cooker and let the dish rest. Cut the dish into the squares and serve.

Nutrition: calories 310, fat 11.7, fiber 5.9, carbs 11.1, protein 40.5

Sweet Mackerel

Prep time: 10 minutes| **Cook time:** 28 minutes| **Servings:** 5

Ingredients:

- 1 teaspoon Erythritol
- 2 tablespoons water
- ¼ cup cream
- 1 pound mackerel
- 1 teaspoon ground white pepper
- 3 tablespoons oregano
- 1 teaspoon olive oil
- ¼ cup of water
- ¼ teaspoon cinnamon

Directions:

Chop the mackerel roughly and sprinkle it with the water, Erythritol, ground white pepper, olive oil, and cinnamon and stir well. Place the fish mixture into the pressure cooker. Add water and close the lid. Cook the dish on "Sauté" mode for 20 minutes. Do not stir the dish during the cooking. When the cooking time ends, remove the dish from the pressure cooker. Transfer to serving plates and serve.

Nutrition: calories 263, fat 18.1, fiber 1.3, carbs 3.3, protein 22.1

Fish Tacos

Prep time: 10 minutes| **Cook time:** 10 minutes| **Servings:** 7

Ingredients:

- 7 almond tortilla
- 8 ounces salmon
- 2 red onions
- 2 red bell peppers
- 1 tablespoon mustard
- 1 tablespoon mayo sauce
- 1 garlic clove
- 2 tablespoons olive oil
- 1 teaspoon sesame seeds
- 1 teaspoon salt
- ¼ cup lettuce

Directions:

Combine mustard with the mayo sauce in a bowl and stir well. Sprinkle the salmon with the mustard sauce and coat the fish well. Set the pressure cooker to "Steam" mode. Spray the pressure cooker with the olive oil. Add the salmon into the pressure cooker and close the lid. Cook the fish for 10 minutes. Meanwhile, remove the seeds from the bell peppers. Cut the bell peppers into strips. Peel the onion and slice it. Tear the lettuce. Peel the garlic and mince the cloves. Sprinkle the tortilla shell with the minced garlic, salt, sesame seeds, and olive oil. Add the bell pepper strips, sliced onions, and lettuce to the tortilla. When the salmon is cooked, remove it from the pressure cooker. Shred the salmon and put it in the tortilla and wrap the tacos.

Nutrition: calories 160, fat 9.8, fiber 2.5, carbs 8.7, protein 10.6

Mussel Soup

Prep time: 10 minutes| **Cook time:** 8 minutes| **Servings:** 6

Ingredients:

- 1 cup cream
- 3 cups chicken stock
- 2 tablespoons olive oil
- 8 ounces mussels
- 1 tablespoon minced garlic
- ½ chili paper
- 1 teaspoon red chile flakes
- 1 onion
- ½ tablespoon salt
- ½ cup parsley
- 7 ounces shallot
- 1 tablespoon lime juice
- 1 teaspoon black-eyed peas

Directions:

Peel the onion and slice it. Chop the shallot and parsley. Set the pressure cooker to "Sauté" mode. Pour the olive oil into the pressure cooker. Add the shallot. A and onion into the pressure cooker and cook the dish on a dish for 4 minutes, stirring frequently. Add chicken stock, cream, minced garlic, chili flakes, salt, lime juice, and black-eyed peas. Add mussels and sprinkle the mixture with the chopped parsley. Close the pressure cooker lid. Set the pressure cooker to "Pressure" mode. Cook the dish for 4 minutes. When the cooking time ends, release the pressure and open the pressure cooker lid. Ladle the mussel soup into serving bowls.

Nutrition: calories 231, fat 14.7, fiber 1, carbs 15.63, protein 10

Chapter 6: Vegetables Recipes

Lime Cabbage and Bacon

Bacon tastes great. And now with the introduction of lime cabbage, it tastes even more sweet.

Prep time: 5 minutes| **Cook time:** 20 minutes| **Servings:** 4

Ingredients:

- 4 cups red cabbage, shredded
- ¼ cup veggie stock
- A pinch of salt and black pepper
- 1 tablespoon olive oil
- 1 cup canned tomatoes, crushed
- Zest of 1 lime, grated
- 2 ounces bacon, cooked and crumbled

Directions:

1. Put the reversible rack in the Foodi, add the baking pan inside and grease it with the oil.
2. Add the cabbage, the stock and the other ingredients into the pan and cook on Baking mode at 380 degrees F for 20 minutes.
3. Divide the mix between plates and serve.

Nutrition: calories 144, fat 3g, carbs 4.5g, protein 4.4g

Potatoes and Lemon Sauce

Are you craving for special-made potatoes? Then, this is the recipe you have been looking for. This recipe will satisfy your hungry family and is full of nutrients.

Prep time: 5 minutes| **Cook time:** 15 minutes| **Servings:** 4

Ingredients:

- 1-pound gold potatoes, peeled and cut into wedges
- 1 tablespoon dill, chopped
- 1 tablespoon lemon zest, grated
- Juice of ½ lemon
- 2 tablespoons butter, melted
- Salt and black pepper to the taste

Directions:

1. Set the Foodi on Sauté mode, add the butter, melt it, add the potatoes and brown for 5 minutes.
2. Add the lemon zest and the other ingredients, set the machine on Air Crisp and cook at 390 degrees F for 10 minutes.
3. Divide everything between plates and serve.

Nutrition: calories 122, fat 3.3g, carbs 3g. protein 2g

Soy Kale

Any time is the best time to enjoy some tasty soy kale. It will satisfy hunger pangs at the right moments.

Prep time: 5 minutes| **Cook time:** 15 minutes| **Servings:** 4

Ingredients:

- 2 pounds kale, torn
- ½ cup soy sauce
- 1 teaspoon honey
- 2 teaspoons olive oil
- ½ teaspoon garlic powder
- Salt and black pepper

Directions:

1. In your Foodi, combine the kale with the soy sauce and the other ingredients, put the pressure lid on and cook on High for 15 minutes.
2. Release the pressure fast for 5 minutes, divide everything between plates and serve.

Nutrition: calories 120, fat 3.5g, carbs 3.3g, protein 1.1g

Chili Eggplant and Kale

This dish poses as a faux lasagna but is cheesy tasty to the core. In 15 minutes or less, it gets ready and is perfect to enjoy by itself, or you may add it as a side to a meat dish.

Prep time: 5 minutes| **Cook time:** 15 minutes| **Servings:** 4

Ingredients:

- Juice of 1 lime
- 1-pound eggplant, roughly cubed
- 1 cup kale, torn
- A pinch of salt and black pepper
- ½ teaspoon chili powder
- ½ cup chicken stock
- 3 tablespoons olive oil

Directions:

1. Set the Foodi on Sauté mode, add the oil, heat it up, add the eggplant and sauté for 2 minutes.

2. Add the kale and the rest of the ingredients, put the pressure lid on and cook on and cook on High for 13 minutes.

3. Release the pressure fast for 5 minutes, divide the mix between plates and serve.

Nutrition: calories 110, fat 3g, carbs 4.3g, protein 1.1g

Minty Radishes

You can't get enough of the creamy, tasty goodness that this recipe has to offer. You've just got to love-it!

Prep time: 5 minutes| **Cook time:** 15 minutes| **Servings:** 4

Ingredients:

- 1-pound radishes, halved
- salt and black pepper
- 2 tablespoons balsamic vinegar
- 2 tablespoon mint, chopped
- 2 tablespoons olive oil

Directions:

1. In your Foodi's basket, combine the radishes with the vinegar and the other ingredients, and cook on Air Crisp at 380 degrees F for 15 minutes.

2. Divide the radishes between plates and serve.

Nutrition: calories 170, fat 4.5g, carbs 7.4g, protein 4.6g

Parsley Kale and Leeks

This recipe is perfectly cooked to bring out the sweet flavors and healthy nutrients in its ingredients. It is filled with lots of flavor and healthy fats and the texture is just right.

Prep time: 5 minutes| **Cook time:** 15 minutes| **Servings:** 4

Ingredients:

- 1-pound kale, torn
- 2 leeks, sliced
- 2 tablespoons balsamic vinegar
- 1 tablespoon parsley, chopped
- Salt and black pepper to the taste
- 2 shallots, chopped
- ½ cup tomato sauce

Directions:

1. In your Foodi, combine the kale with the leeks and the other ingredients, put the pressure lid on and cook on High for 15 minutes.

2. Release the pressure fast for 5 minutes, divide the mix between plates and serve.

Nutrition: calories 100, fat 2g, carbs 3.4g, protein 4g

Carrots and Walnuts Salad

Fun fact here: carrots, and walnuts are given an aromatic kick. With this, your meaty plates just got a lot more pleasant. Make sure to cook them not to be too wilted so that you can enjoy some crunch with as you bite on.

Prep time: 5 minutes| **Cook time:** 15 minutes| **Servings:** 4

Ingredients:

- 4 carrots, roughly shredded
- ½ cup walnuts, sliced
- 3 tablespoons balsamic vinegar
- 1 cup chicken stock
- Salt and black pepper to the taste
- 1 tablespoon olive oil

Directions:

1. In your Foodi, mix the carrots with the vinegar and the other ingredients except the walnuts, put the pressure lid on and cook on High for 15 minutes.

2. Release the pressure fast for 5 minutes, divide the mix between plates and serve with the walnuts sprinkled on top.

Nutrition: calories 120, fat 4.5g, carbs 5.3g, protein 1.3g

Pine Nuts Okra and Leeks

It is made few ingredients and is very delicious. If you are craving a perfect veggie snack, then this is the perfect one for you. It is easy to make and you will love this mouthwatering delicacy.

Prep time: 5 minutes| **Cook time:** 12 minutes| **Servings:** 4

Ingredients:

- 1-pound okra, trimmed
- 2 leeks, sliced
- Salt and black pepper to the taste
- 1 cup tomato sauce
- ¼ cup pine nuts, toasted
- 1 tablespoon cilantro, chopped

Directions:

1. In your Foodi, mix the okra with the leeks and the other ingredients except the cilantro, put the pressure lid on and cook on High for 12 minutes.

2. Release the pressure fast for 5 minutes, divide the okra mix into bowls and serve with the cilantro sprinkled on top.

Nutrition: calories 146, fat 3g, carbs 4g, protein 3g

Sesame Radish and Leeks

Sesame Radish and Leeks recipe is filled with lots of flavors. It is easy and quick to make as you need only 15 minutes to cook it! You will enjoy its good taste and healthy nutrients.

Prep time: 5 minutes| **Cook time:** 15 minutes| **Servings:** 4

Ingredients:

- 2 leeks, sliced
- ½ pound radishes, sliced
- 2 scallions, chopped
- 2 tablespoons black sesame seeds
- 1|3 cup chicken stock
- 1 tablespoon ginger, grated
- 1 tablespoon chives, minced

Directions:

1. In your Foodi, combine the leeks with the radishes and the other ingredients, put the pressure lid on and cook on High for 15 minutes more.

2. Release the pressure fast for 5 minutes, divide everything between plates and serve.

Nutrition: calories 112, fat 2g, carbs 4.2g, protein 2g

Lime Broccoli and Cauliflower

Make this crunchy recipe as often as you can to go with the different sauces and meat dishes that are shared here.

Prep time: 10 minutes| **Cook time:** 15 minutes| **Servings:** 4

Ingredients:

- 2 cups broccoli florets
- 1 cup cauliflower florets
- 2 tablespoons lime juice
- 1 tablespoon avocado oil
- 1|3 cup tomato sauce
- 2 teaspoons ginger, grated
- 2 teaspoons garlic, minced
- 1 tablespoon chives, chopped

Directions:

1. Set the Foodi on Sauté mode, add the oil, heat it up, add the garlic and the ginger and sauté for 2 minutes.

2. Add the broccoli, cauliflower and the rest of the ingredients, put the pressure lid on and cook on High for 13 minutes.

3. Release the pressure naturally for 10 minutes, divide everything between plates and serve.

Nutrition: calories 118, fat 1.5g, carbs 4.3g, protein 6g

Napa Cabbage and Carrots

This recipe is easily fixed and takes just 20 minutes to cook and 5 minutes for preparation.

Prep time: 5 minutes| **Cook time:** 20 minutes| **Servings:** 4

Ingredients:

- 1 Napa cabbage, shredded
- 2 carrots, sliced
- 2 tablespoons olive oil
- 1 red onion, chopped
- Salt and black pepper to the taste
- 2 tablespoons sweet paprika
- ½ cup tomato sauce

Directions:

1. Set the Foodi on Sauté mode, add the oil, heat it up, add the onion and sauté for 5 minutes.

2. Add the carrots, the cabbage and the other ingredients, toss, put the pressure lid on and cook on High for 15 minutes.

3. Release the pressure fast for 5 minutes, divide everything between plates and serve.

Nutrition: calories 140, fat 3.4g, carbs 1.2g, protein 3.5 g

Zucchinis and Spinach Mix

This recipe is a great meal for a date night. It is quite easy and quick to prepare. It is full of flavor and you and your partner will enjoy it all the way!

Prep time: 5 minutes| **Cook time:** 17 minutes| **Servings:** 4

Ingredients:

- 2 zucchinis, sliced
- 1-pound baby spinach
- ½ cup tomato sauce
- Salt and black pepper
- 1 tablespoon avocado oil
- 1 red onion, chopped
- 1 tablespoon sweet paprika
- ½ teaspoon garlic powder
- ½ teaspoon chili powder

Directions:

1. Set the Foodi on Sauté, add the oil, heat it up, add the onion and sauté for 2 minutes.

2. Add the zucchinis, spinach, and the other ingredients, put the pressure lid on and cook on High for 15 minutes.

3. Release the pressure fast for 5 minutes, divide everything between plates and serve.

Nutrition: calories 130, fat 5.5g, carbs 3.3g, protein 1g

Creamy Kale

It is amazingly delicious and filled with lots of flavors. it can be eaten with quite a range of raw veggies therefore making it versatile.

Prep time: 5 minutes| **Cook time:** 15 minutes| **Servings:** 4

Ingredients:

- 1 tablespoon lemon juice
- 2 tablespoons balsamic vinegar
- 1-pound kale, torn
- 1 tablespoon ginger, grated
- 1 garlic clove, minced
- 2 tablespoons olive oil
- 1 cup heavy cream
- A pinch of salt and black pepper
- 2 tablespoons chives, chopped

Directions:

1. Set the Foodi on Sauté mode, add the oil, heat it up, add the garlic and the ginger and sauté for 2 minutes.

2. Add the kale, lemon juice and the other ingredients, put the pressure lid on and cook on High for 13 minutes.

3. Release the pressure fast for 5 minutes, divide between plates and serve.

Nutrition: calories 130, fat 2g, carbs 3.4g, protein 2g

Radish and Apples Mix

This mix is good and can be taken as a snack and a main meal. You will love it.

Prep time: 5 minutes| **Cook time:** 15 minutes| **Servings:** 4

Ingredients:

- 1-pound radishes, roughly cubed
- 2 green apples, cored and cut into wedges
- ¼ cup chicken stock
- 2 spring onions, chopped
- 3 tablespoons tomato paste
- Juice of 1 lime
- Cooking spray
- 1 tablespoon cilantro, chopped

Directions:

1. In your Foodi, combine the radishes with the apples and the other ingredients, put the pressure lid on and cook on High for 15 minutes.

2. Release the pressure fast for 5 minutes, divide everything between plates and serve.

Nutrition: calories 122, fat 5g, carbs 4.5g, protein 3g

Pomegranate Radish Mix

Pomegranate Radish Mix is full of sweet flavor and takes only 8 minutes to cook which is not much time and therefore it be considered a quick fix.

Prep time: 5 minutes| **Cook time:** 8 minutes| **Servings:** 4

Ingredients:

- 1-pound radishes, roughly cubed
- Salt and black pepper to the taste
- 2 garlic cloves, minced
- ½ cup chicken stock
- 2 tablespoons pomegranate juice
- ¼ cup pomegranate seeds

Directions:

1. In your Foodi, combine the radishes with the stock and the other ingredients, put the pressure lid on and cook on High for 8 minutes.

2. Release the pressure fast for 5 minutes, divide everything between plates and serve.

Nutrition: calories 133, fat 2.3g, carbs 2.4g, protein 2g

Garlic Red Bell Peppers Mix

This tasty Garlic Red Bell Peppers Mix can be enjoyed at any time. I reckon it will satisfy hunger pangs at the right moments.

Prep time: 5 minutes| **Cook time:** 16 minutes| **Servings:** 4

Ingredients:

- 1-pound red bell peppers, cut into wedges
- ½ teaspoon curry powder
- ½ cup tomato sauce
- Salt and black pepper to the taste
- 1 tablespoon olive oil
- 2 garlic cloves, minced
- 1 tablespoon parsley, chopped

Directions:

1. Put the reversible rack in the Foodi, add the baking pan inside and grease it with the oil.
2. Add the peppers, curry powder and the other ingredients except the parsley, toss a bit and cook on Baking mode at 380 degrees F for 16 minutes.
3. Divide between plates and serve with the parsley sprinkled on top.

Nutrition: calories 150, fat 3.5g, carbs 3.1g, protein 1.2g

Chives Beets and Carrots

Super packed with richness: proteins, vitamins, and healthy fats. This recipe is so filling and delicious.

Prep time: 5 minutes| **Cook time:** 20 minutes| **Servings:** 4

Ingredients:

- 1-pound beets, peeled and roughly cubed
- 1-pound baby carrots, peeled
- Salt and black pepper to the taste
- 2 tablespoons olive oil
- 1 tablespoon chives, minced

Directions:

1. In a bowl, mix the beets with the carrots and the other ingredients and toss.
2. Put the beets and carrots in the Foodie's basket, cook on Air Crisp at 390 degrees F for 20 minutes, divide between plates and serve.

Nutrition: calories 150, fat 4.5g, carbs 7.3g, protein 3.6g

Balsamic Cabbage and Endives

This recipe is tasty, fresh and so delicious. It is also easy to make and has lots of nutrients which are good for you. It can made for your family or your guests.

Prep time: 5 minutes| **Cook time:** 15 minutes| **Servings:** 4

Ingredients:

- 1 green cabbage head, shredded
- 2 endives, trimmed and sliced lengthwise
- Salt and black pepper to the taste
- 1 tablespoon olive oil
- 2 shallots, chopped
- ½ cup chicken stock
- 1 tablespoon sweet paprika
- 1 tablespoon balsamic vinegar

Directions:

1. Set the Foodi on Sauté mode, add the oil, heat it up, add the shallots and sauté for 2 minutes.
2. Add the cabbage, the endives and the other ingredients, put the pressure lid on and cook on High for 13 minutes.
3. Release the pressure fast for 5 minutes, divide the mix between plates and serve.

Nutrition: calories 120, fat 2g, carbs 3.3g, protein 4

Lemony Leeks and Carrots

The ingredients of this recipe nourishing and simple. They also taste so well. It only has few ingredients which also means that it can be fixed easily and quickly.

Prep time: 5 minutes| **Cook time:** 15 minutes| **Servings:** 4

Ingredients:

- 2 leeks, roughly sliced
- 2 carrots, sliced
- 1 teaspoon ginger powder
- 1 teaspoon garlic powder
- ½ cup chicken stock
- Salt and black pepper to the taste
- 2 tablespoons lemon juice
- 2 tablespoons olive oil
- ½ tablespoon balsamic vinegar

Directions:

1. In your Foodi, combine the leeks with the carrots and the other ingredients, put the pressure lid on and cook on High for 15 minutes.

2. Release the pressure fast for 5 minutes, divide the mix between plates and serve.

Nutrition: calories 133, fat 3.4g, carbs 5g, protein 2.1g

Kale and Parmesan

This recipe is very simple and easy to prepare. It is a delicious recipe that has lots of flavors. It is very nutritious and a good protein source.

Prep time: 5 minutes| **Cook time:** 15 minutes| **Servings:** 4

Ingredients:

- 1-pound kale, torn
- 2 tablespoons parmesan, grated
- 1 red onion, sliced
- 1 cup bacon, cooked and chopped
- ½ cup chicken stock
- 1 tablespoon olive oil
- A pinch of salt and black pepper
- 1 tablespoon balsamic vinegar

Directions:

1. Set the Foodi on Sauté mode, add the oil, heat it up, add the onion and sauté for 2 minutes.

2. Add the kale and the other ingredients except the parmesan.

3. Sprinkle the cheese at the end, set the machine on Baking mode and cook at 380 degrees F for 12 minutes.

4. Divide everything into bowls and serve.

Nutrition: calories 130, fat 5g, carbs 3.4g, protein 6g

Chapter 7: Side Dishes Recipes

Zucchini Noodles

Prep time: 10 minutes| **Cook time:** 10 minutes| **Servings:** 6

Ingredients:

- 2 medium green zucchini
- 1 tablespoon wine vinegar
- 1 teaspoon white pepper
- ½ teaspoon cilantro
- ¼ teaspoon nutmeg
- 1 cup chicken stock
- 1 garlic clove

Directions:

Wash the zucchini and use a spiralizer to make the zucchini noodles. Peel the garlic and chop it. Combine the cilantro, chopped garlic clove, nutmeg, and white pepper together in a mixing bowl. Sprinkle the zucchini noodles with the spice mixture. Pour the chicken stock in the pressure cooker and sauté the liquid on the manual mode until it is become to boil. Add the zucchini noodles and wine vinegar and stir the mixture gently. Cook for 3 minutes on the "Sauté" mode. Remove the zucchini noodles from the pressure cooker and serve.

Nutrition: calories 28, fat 0.7, fiber 1, carbs 3.94, protein 2

Wrapped Asparagus

Prep time: 10 minutes| **Cook time:** 7 minutes| **Servings:** 4

Ingredients:

- 1-pound asparagus
- 7 oz bacon, sliced
- ½ teaspoon salt
- 1 teaspoon olive oil
- ½ teaspoon cayenne pepper

Directions:

Sprinkle the sliced bacon with salt, cayenne pepper, and olive oil. Then wrap asparagus into the sliced bacon and place in the cooker basket. Lower the air fryer lid and cook the side dish for 7 minutes. The cooked meal should have crispy bacon.

Nutrition: calories 302, fat 22.1, fiber 2.4, carbs 5.2, protein 20.9

Cabbage Hash Brown

Prep time: 15 minutes| **Cook time:** 13 minutes| **Servings:** 6

Ingredients:

- 1-pound white cabbage, shredded
- 1 white onion, diced
- 1 tablespoon apple cider vinegar
- 1 teaspoon salt
- 1 teaspoon ground black pepper
- 3 oz bacon, chopped
- 1 cup heavy cream
- ½ cup of water
- ½ teaspoon tomato paste
- 1 teaspoon paprika
- 1 garlic clove, diced
- 1 oz pork rinds

Directions:

1. Put the shredded cabbage in the mixing bowl. Sprinkle it with apple cider vinegar, salt, ground black pepper, and paprika. Mix up well and leave the mixture for 10 minutes.

2. After this, transfer it in the cooker. Add chopped bacon, heavy cream, water, tomato paste, garlic clove, and pork rinds. Mix it up carefully and close the lid. Cook the hash brown on High-pressure mode for 13 minutes. Then allow natural pressure release for 10 minutes. Open the lid and mix up the meal well.

Nutrition: calories 202, fat 15.2, fiber 2.5, carbs 7.6, protein 10

Red Beetroot Salad

Prep time: 10 minutes| **Cook time:** 35 minutes| **Servings:** 7

Ingredients:

- 1 pound beetroot
- 1 red onion
- 3 tablespoons sunflower oil
- 1 tablespoon pumpkin seeds
- 8 ounces feta cheese
- 1 tablespoon basil
- ½ cup fresh parsley
- 4 cups of water

Directions:

Peel the beetroot and place it in the pressure cooker. Add water and close the lid. Cook the beetroot on manual mode for 35 minutes. Meanwhile, peel the onion and slice it. Crumble the cheese and chop the parsley. When the beetroot is cooked, remove it from the pressure cooker and chill well. Chop it into the medium cubes. Combine the beetroot with the sliced onion. Add pumpkin seeds and crumbled feta cheese. Sprinkle the mixture with basil and sunflower oil. Stir the salad well and transfer it to serving plate.

Nutrition: calories 180, fat 13.6, fiber 2, carbs 9.42, protein 6

Mashed Turnips with Chives

Prep time: 10 minutes| **Cook time:** 6 minutes| **Servings:** 4

Ingredients:

- 2 cups turnips, peeled, chopped
- 2 tablespoons chives, chopped
- 1 tablespoon butter
- 3 cups of water
- 1 teaspoon salt
- 1 teaspoon garlic powder

Directions:

Put turnip in the cooker. Add water and salt. Cook it on High-pressure mode for 6 minutes. Then use quick pressure release. Open the lid and drain water. Transfer turnip into the food processor. Add butter and garlic powder. Blend it until you get smooth mash. Transfer the turnip mash in the serving bowls and sprinkle with chives. Mix up the meal gently.

Nutrition: calories 63, fat 2.9, fiber 2.1, carbs 8.6, protein 1.2

Butternut Squash with Garlic

Prep time: 10 minutes| **Cook time:** 15 minutes| **Servings:** 4

Ingredients:

- 1 pound butternut squash
- 1 tablespoon minced garlic
- 3 tablespoons butter
- ½ teaspoon white pepper
- 1 teaspoon paprika
- 1 teaspoon olive oil
- 1 teaspoon turmeric

Directions:

Wash the squash and make the thin incisions. Melt the butter and combine it with the minced garlic and stir the mixture. Spray the pressure cooker with the olive oil inside. Place the squash in the pressure cooker. Sprinkle the squash with turmeric and paprika. Top it with garlic butter. Close the lid and cook the dish on the "Pressure" mode for 15 minutes. When the cooking time ends, the butternut squash should be soft. Remove it from the pressure cooker and let it cool briefly before serving.

Nutrition: calories 145, fat 10, fiber 3, carbs 14.99, protein 2

Sweet Glazed Onion

Prep time: 5 minutes| **Cook time:** 12 minutes| **Servings:** 6

Ingredients:

- 1 pound white onions
- 3 tablespoons butter
- ⅓ cup Erythritol
- 1 teaspoon thyme
- ½ teaspoon white pepper
- 1 tablespoon paprika
- ¼ cup cream

Directions:

Peel the onions and slice them. Sprinkle the sliced onions with Erythritol. Add thyme, white pepper, and paprika and stir the mixture. Place the onion mixture in the pressure cooker. Add butter and set the pressure cooker to "Sauté" mode and sauté the mixture for 7 minutes. Stir it frequently using a wooden spoon. Add cream and blend well. Close the lid and cook the glazed onion at the pressure mode for 5 minutes. Remove the cooked onions from the pressure cooker, allow it to rest briefly before serving.

Nutrition: calories 92, fat 6.6, fiber 2.2, carbs 8.2, protein 1.2

Cabbage Rice

Prep time: 15 minutes| **Cook time:** 3 minutes| **Servings:** 2

Ingredients:

- 8 oz white cabbage
- ½ cup of water
- ¾ cup cream
- 1 teaspoon salt

Directions:

Shred the cabbage until you get the cabbage rice mixture. Add salt and mix up it well. Then transfer the cabbage rice in the Pressure cooker. Add water and cream. Mix it up. Close and seal the lid. Cook the cabbage rice for 3 minutes on High-pressure mode. Then allow natural pressure release for 10 minutes. Open the lid and transfer hot cabbage rice into the serving bowls.

Nutrition: calories 86, fat 5.1, fiber 2.8, carbs 9.4, protein 2.2

Sautéed Spinach

Prep time: 10 minutes| **Cook time:** 13 minutes| **Servings:** 5

Ingredients:

- 3 cups spinach
- 1 cup half and half
- 1 teaspoon olive oil
- 1 teaspoon cilantro
- ½ teaspoon rosemary
- 1 tablespoon butter
- 1 teaspoon kosher salt
- 1 lemon

Directions:

Wash the spinach and chop it. Pour olive oil into the pressure cooker and preheat it on the "Sauté" mode. Transfer the chopped spinach in the pressure cooker. Sprinkle it with kosher salt, rosemary, and cilantro. Stir the mixture and sauté it for 3 minutes. Stir the mixture frequently. Add the butter and half and a half. Close the lid and cook the spinach on the "Sauté" mode for 10 minutes. Squeeze the lemon juice onto the spinach and mix well. Remove the dish from the pressure cooker and rest briefly. Transfer it to serving plates.

Nutrition: calories 99, fat 8.9, fiber 0.8, carbs 3.9, protein 2.1

Carrot Puree

Prep time: 15 minutes| **Cook time:** 25 minutes| **Servings:** 6

Ingredients:

- 5 medium carrots
- ½ cup of water
- ½ cup of orange juice
- 1 teaspoon butter
- ½ teaspoon cinnamon

Directions:

Wash the carrots and peel them. Slice the carrots and place them in a mixing bowl. Sprinkle the vegetables with cinnamon and mix well. Leave the mixture for 10 minutes to get the carrot juice. Transfer the mixture with the liquid in the pressure cooker. Add water and orange juice. Close the lid, and set the pressure cooker mode to "Sauté." Cook for 25 minutes or until the carrots are soft. Let the carrots rest briefly and transfer the mixture to a blender. Blend well until smooth. Add butter and stir. Serve the carrot puree warm.

Nutrition: calories 36, fat 0.7, fiber 1.4, carbs 7.3, protein 0.6

Keto Tortillas

Prep time: 10 minutes| **Cook time:** 6 minutes| **Servings:** 4

Ingredients:

- 1 cup almond flour
- ½ cup coconut flour
- ½ teaspoon salt
- 3 tablespoons olive oil
- ½ cup of water

Directions:

In the mixing bowl, mix up together almond flour, coconut flour, salt, and water. Stir the mixture with the help of spoon|fork until it is homogenous. Then add olive oil and knead a non-sticky soft dough. Cut it into 4 pieces. Roll up every dough piece with the help of the rolling pin. In the end, you should get 4 rounds (tortillas). Preheat cooker on saute mode well. Place 1 tortilla in the cooker and cook it for 1 minute from each side. Repeat the same steps with the remaining tortillas. Cover the cooked tortillas with the towel to save them fresh.

Nutrition: calories 330, fat 27.5, fiber 8, carbs 13, protein 2

Creamed Onions Halves

Prep time: 10 minutes| **Cook time:** 25 minutes| **Servings:** 10

Ingredients:

- 1 cup cream
- 1 cup of coconut milk
- 6 big white onions
- 1 teaspoon ground black pepper
- ½ tablespoon salt
- 1 tablespoon paprika
- ½ cup fresh dill
- ½ cup basil
- 1 tablespoon cilantro
- 1 teaspoon mint
- 1 teaspoon minced garlic

Directions:

Peel the onions and slice them into thick slices. Place the sliced onion in the pressure cooker. Combine the coconut milk and cream together in a mixing bowl. Add ground black pepper, salt, and paprika and stir the mixture. Add the cilantro, mint, and minced garlic. Stir the mixture well. Pour the cream mixture onto the onion slices. Wash the fresh dill and basil and chop them. Sprinkle the onions with the chopped seasonings. Close the pressure cooker lid, and set the pressure cooker mode to "Sauté". Cook the onions for 25 minutes or until soft. Release the pressure and open the pressure cooker lid. Transfer the onions in the serving plates and sprinkle them with the gravy.

Nutrition: calories 116, fat 7.4, fiber 3.2, carbs 12.5, protein 2.4

Green Asian-style Zucchini Strips

Prep time: 10 minutes| **Cook time:** 5 minutes| **Servings:** 6

Ingredients:

- 2 tablespoons sesame oil
- 3 green zucchini
- 1 tablespoon cilantro
- 1 teaspoon basil
- 1 tablespoon kosher salt
- 1 tablespoon butter
- ½ cup pork rinds
- ½ cup of coconut milk
- 4 eggs
- 1 tablespoon cumin

Directions:

Wash the zucchini and cut them into the strips. Place the zucchini strips in the mixing bowl. Sprinkle them with the kosher salt, basil, and cilantro and stir the mixture. Pour the sesame oil in the pressure cooker and preheat it on the "Sauté" mode. Combine the eggs and coconut milk and whisk the mixture. Dip the zucchini strips in the egg mixture. Coat the vegetables in the pork rind. Place the zucchini strips in the pressure cooker and sauté them for 1 minute on each side. Sprinkle the dish with cumin and serve.

Nutrition: calories 225, fat 18.5, fiber 1.6, carbs 3.8, protein 12.4

Japanese Style Black Bean Pasta

Prep time: 10 minutes| **Cook time:** 8 minutes| **Servings:** 6

Ingredients:

- 7 oz black beans pasta
- 1 cup of water
- 1 tablespoon rice vinegar
- 1 teaspoon Erythritol
- 1 teaspoon sesame seeds
- 1 teaspoon red chili flakes
- 1 teaspoon salt

Directions:

Place black beans pasta in the cooker. Add water, salt, and chili flakes. Close and seal the lid. Cook the pasta for 8 minutes in High-pressure mode. Then use quick pressure release and open the lid. Drain water and transfer pasta in the bowl. In the separated bowl, mix up together rice vinegar, Erythritol, and sesame seeds. Stir gently. Add the mixture into the pasta and shake gently. Transfer the meal into the serving bowls.

Nutrition: calories 111, fat 1.4, fiber 7.2, carbs 10.2, protein 14.9

Cream Spinach

Prep time: 10 minutes| **Cook time:** 10 minutes| **Servings:** 4

Ingredients:

- 4 cups spinach, chopped
- 1 tablespoon butter
- 1 cup cream
- 1 teaspoon salt
- 4 oz Cheddar cheese, shredded
- 1 teaspoon cayenne pepper
- 1 teaspoon paprika
- 1 tablespoon olive oil

Directions:

Pour cream in the cooker. Add salt, butter, cayenne pepper, and paprika. Preheat it on saute mode. When the liquid starts to boil, add chopped spinach. Stir well and saute the greens for 5 minutes. After this, sprinkle the spinach with shredded cheese and stir well. Close the lid and saute the meal for 5 minutes more. Switch off Ninja Pressure cooker and open the lid. Mix up the spinach well.

Nutrition: calories 218, fat 19.4, fiber 1, carbs 3.9, protein 8.6

Balsamic Onions

Prep time: 10 minutes| **Cook time:** 17 minutes| **Servings:** 4

Ingredients:

- 4 medium white onion
- 1 tablespoon ground black pepper
- 2 tablespoons lemon juice
- 1 tablespoon apple cider vinegar
- 1 teaspoon Erythritol
- ½ teaspoon salt
- ½ teaspoon oregano
- 1 tablespoon olive oil

Directions:

Peel the onions and chop the vegetables roughly. Combine the ground black pepper, Erythritol, salt, and oregano together in a mixing bowl and stir the mixture. Sprinkle the chopped onions with the spice mixture and stir using your hands. Add the onions to the pressure cooker. Sprinkle the mixture with the olive oil and set the pressure cooker to "Sauté" mode. Sauté the onions for 10 minutes. Stir them frequently. Add apple cider vinegar and lemon juice, stir the mixture and sauté the dish for 7 minutes with the lid closed. Remove the dish from the pressure cooker, let it rest briefly, and serve.

Nutrition: calories 81, fat 3.7, fiber 2.9, carbs 11.6, protein 1.5

Turmeric Mushroom Hats

Prep time: 15 minutes| **Cook time:** 25 minutes| **Servings:** 6

Ingredients:

- 2 tablespoons turmeric
- 1 tablespoon garlic powder
- 1 teaspoon minced garlic
- 1 teaspoon of sea salt
- ½ cup parsley
- 1 tablespoon olive oil
- 1 tablespoon butter
- 10 ounces large mushroom caps

Directions:

Wash the mushroom caps and remove the stems and gills. Wash the parsley and chop it with the mushroom stems. Place the parsley in a blender and pulse several times. Transfer the blended parsley in the mixing bowl. Add butter, minced garlic, sea salt, garlic powder, and turmeric. Stir the mixture well until smooth. Fill the mushroom caps with the parsley mixture. Spray the pressure cooker with the olive oil inside and transfer the mushroom hat there. Close the lid and cook on the "Sear/sauté" mode for 25 minutes. When the cooking time ends, open the lid and leave the mushroom caps in the machine for 5 minutes. Remove the mushroom caps from the pressure cooker and serve.

Nutrition: calories 66, fat 4.5, fiber 0.8, carbs 4.3, protein 2

Spaghetti Squash

Prep time: 15 minutes| **Cook time:** 10 minutes| **Servings:** 3

Ingredients:

- 10 oz spaghetti squash
- 1 tablespoon butter
- 1 teaspoon ground black pepper
- 1 cup water, for cooking

Directions:

Pour water in the cooker and insert trivet inside. Cut the spaghetti squash into halves and remove seeds. Place the squash on the trivet. Close and seal the lid. Cook the vegetable on High-pressure mode 10 minutes. Then make a quick pressure release. Open the lid. Transfer the spaghetti squash on the plate and shred the flesh with the help of the fork. You will get the spaghetti shape mixture. Sprinkle it with ground black pepper and add butter. Stir it well. It is recommended to serve the side dish warm or hot.

Nutrition: calories 65, fat 4.4, fiber 0.2, carbs 7, protein 0.7

Shumai

Prep time: 20 minutes| **Cook time:** 10 minutes| **Servings:** 7

Ingredients:

- 6 ounces wonton wraps
- 1 cup ground beef
- 6 ounces tiger shrimp
- 1 teaspoon salt
- 2 tablespoons fish sauce
- ⅓ cup of soy sauce
- 1 teaspoon ground ginger
- 1 teaspoon white pepper
- 1 teaspoon salt
- ½ teaspoon cilantro
- 3 ounces green onions
- 1 teaspoon oregano
- 2 teaspoons ground white pepper

Directions:

Combine the ground beef, salt, cilantro, and oregano together. Mince the tiger shrimp. Combine the minced shrimp with the ground white pepper. Chop the green onion and add it to the shrimp mixture. Add the fish sauce, soy sauce, and ground ginger. Combine the shrimp mixture and the ground beef mixture together. Mix well until combined completely. Place the meat mixture into the wonton wraps and wrap the shumai to get the open top. Pour water in the pressure cooker. Place the shumai in the steamer and transfer it to the pressure cooker. Close the pressure cooker lid and cook the shumai for 5 minutes at the "Steam" mode. After 10 minutes, release the steam and remove the dish from the pressure cooker and serve.

Nutrition: calories 142, fat 3, fiber 1, carbs 19.68, protein 9

Garlic Cauliflower Florets

Prep time: 15 minutes| **Cook time:** 5 minutes| **Servings:** 6

Ingredients:

- 15 oz cauliflower florets
- 1 teaspoon salt
- 1 tablespoon garlic powder
- 1 tablespoon avocado oil
- 1 teaspoon butter, melted
- ½ teaspoon dried oregano

Directions:

Mix up together salt, garlic powder, avocado oil, melted butter, and dried oregano. Brush every cauliflower floret with the garlic mixture and leave for 10 minutes to marinate. After this, transfer the vegetables in the cooker basket. Sprinkle them with the remaining garlic mixture. Lower the crisp lid and cook the cauliflower for 5 minutes or until it starts to get light brown color and tender texture. Transfer the side dish on the serving plates.

Nutrition: calories 31, fat 1, fiber 2.1, carbs 5, protein 1.7

Tender Collard Greens

Prep time: 10 minutes| **Cook time:** 20 minutes| **Servings:** 2

Ingredients:

- 2 cups collard greens, chopped
- ½ cup of water
- 3 tablespoons heavy cream
- 1 teaspoon salt
- 1 teaspoon paprika
- ¼ cup walnuts, chopped

Directions:

Place collard greens in the cooker. Sprinkle the greens with salt and paprika. Add heavy cream and water. Mix up the greens gently and close the lid. Cook them for 3 minutes on High-pressure mode. Then allow natural pressure release for 10 minutes. Open the lid and add walnuts. Mix up the meal and transfer on the serving plates.

Nutrition: calories 190, fat 18, fiber 3, carbs 5.3, protein 5.4

Celery Root Cubes

Prep time: 10 minutes| **Cook time:** 8 minutes| **Servings:** 6

Ingredients:

- 12 oz celery root, peeled
- 1 teaspoon salt
- 1 teaspoon ground black pepper
- 1 tablespoon butter
- 1 teaspoon olive oil
- 1 teaspoon minced garlic
- 1 tablespoon fresh parsley, chopped
- ¾ cup heavy cream

Directions:

Chop the celery root into medium cubes. Preheat Ninja Cooker on Saute mode well. Then add butter and olive oil. Preheat the mixture. Add chopped celery root, ground black pepper, salt, and minced garlic. Stir well and saute for 5 minutes. After this, add chopped parsley and heavy cream. Stir the mixture well. Close the lid and cook it on High-pressure mode for 3 minutes. Then allow natural pressure release for 10 minutes. Chill the cooked celery cubes till the room temperature.

Nutrition: calories 101, fat 8.4, fiber 1.1, carbs 6.1, protein 1.3

Cauliflower Rice

Prep time: 10 minutes

Cook time: 5 minutes

Servings: 4

Ingredients:

- 1 ½ cup cauliflower
- 1 cup of water
- 1 tablespoon butter
- ¼ cup heavy cream
- 1 tablespoon dried dill
- 1 teaspoon salt

Directions:

Chop the cauliflower roughly and transfer it into the food processor. Blend the vegetables until you gets cauliflower rice. Place the "cauliflower rice" in the cooker. Add butter, salt, dried dill, heavy cream, and water. Close and seal the lid. Cook the meal on High-pressure mode for 5 minutes. Use quick pressure release. Open the lid and stir the cauliflower rice carefully.

Nutrition: calories 63, fat 5.7, fiber 1.1, carbs 2.6, protein 1.1

Broccoli Salad

Prep time: 10 minutes| **Cook time:** 10 minutes| **Servings:** 6

Ingredients:
- 1 white onion
- 1 pound broccoli
- ½ cup chicken stock
- 1 tablespoon salt
- 1 teaspoon olive oil
- 1 teaspoon garlic powder
- 3 tablespoons raisins
- 2 tablespoons walnuts, crushed
- 1 teaspoon oregano
- 1 tablespoon lemon juice

Directions:

Wash the broccoli and separate into small florets. Place the broccoli in the pressure cooker and sprinkle with the salt. Close the lid and cook the vegetables on the "Pressure" mode for 10 minutes. Transfer the broccoli to a serving bowl. Peel the onion and slice it. Add the onion to the broccoli. Sprinkle the mixture with the garlic powder, oregano, crushed walnuts, raisins, and lemon juice. Add olive oil and stir gently before serving.

Nutrition: calories 68, fat 3, fiber 3, carbs 4.09, protein 4

Chapter 8: Desserts Recipes

Chocolate Topping

Prep time: 5 minutes| **Cook time:** 2 minutes| **Servings:** 4

Ingredients:

- 1 tablespoon cocoa powder
- 4 tablespoons butter
- 1 oz dark chocolate
- 1 tablespoon Erythritol

Directions:

Place butter, cocoa powder, and dark chocolate in the Ninja Pressure cooker. Add Erythritol and stir gently. Close the lid and cook the mixture on High-pressure mode for 2 minutes. Then make quick pressure release. Open the lid and whisk the cooked mixture well. Transfer it in the glass jar and store in the fridge up to 3 days.

Nutrition: calories 143, fat 13.8, fiber 0.6, carbs 8, protein 0.9

Blueberry Muffins

Prep time: 15 minutes| **Cook time:** 10 minutes| **Servings:** 6

Ingredients:

- 1 cup frozen blueberries
- 1 ½ cup coconut flour
- 1 teaspoon baking powder
- 1 tablespoon apple cider vinegar
- 1 tablespoon coconut
- ½ cup almond milk
- 2 eggs
- 1 teaspoon vanilla extract
- 1 teaspoon olive oil

Directions:

Place the coconut flour, baking soda, apple cider vinegar, coconut, almond milk, eggs, and vanilla extract in a food processor. Blend the mixture well. Add the frozen blueberries and blend the mixture for 30 seconds more. Take the muffin molds and fill half of every mold with the batter. Place the muffins molds on the trivet and transfer it to the pressure cooker. Close the lid and cook at "Pressure" mode for 10 minutes. When the muffins are baked, remove them from the pressure cooker. Let them rest and serve.

Nutrition: calories 214, fat 10.4, fiber 13.1, carbs 25.4, protein 6.5

Vanilla Ice Cream

Prep time: 10 minutes| **Cook time:** 5 minutes| **Servings:** 4

Ingredients:

- 1 cup heavy cream
- 4 egg yolks
- 3 teaspoons Erythritol
- 1 tablespoon vanilla extract

Directions:

Whisk together Erythritol and egg yolks. Then pour heavy cream in the Ninja Foodie. Add egg yolk mixture and vanilla extract. Cook the liquid on High-pressure mode for 5 minutes. Then make a quick pressure release and open the lid. Stir it well and transfer in the mixing bowl. Mix up the mixture with the help of the hand mixer until it starts to be thick. Then transfer it in the ice cream maker and make ice cream according to the Directions: of the manufacturer.

Nutrition: calories 365, fat 15.6, fiber 0, carbs 5.6, protein 3.3

Chocolate Bacon

Prep time: 10 minutes| **Cook time:** 4 minutes| **Servings:** 6

Ingredients:

- 6 bacon slices
- 2 oz dark chocolate, melted

Directions:

Place the bacon slices in the basket and close the lid. Set the Air fryer mode and cook bacon for 4 minutes. Flip it onto another side after 2 minutes of cooking.

Then dip the cooked bacon in the melted chocolate and let it chill until the chocolate is solid.

Nutrition: calories 156, fat 11.3, fiber 0.5, carbs 4.1, protein 8

Savory Baked Apples

Prep time: 10 minutes| **Cook time:** 15 minutes| **Servings:** 5

Ingredients:

- 5 red apples
- 1 tablespoon stevia, powdered
- ½ cup almonds
- 1 teaspoon cinnamon
- 1 cup of water

Directions:

Wash the apples and cut the tops off. Remove the seeds and flesh from the apples to make apple cups. Crush the almonds. Sprinkle the apples with the cinnamon and stevia. Fill the apples with the almond mixture and cover them with the apple tops. Pour water in the pressure cooker. Add the stuffed apples and close the pressure cooker lid. Cook the apples at "Sauté" mode for 15 minutes. When the cooking time ends, transfer the apples to a serving plate.

Nutrition: calories 172, fat 5.2, fiber 6.8, carbs 33.2, protein 2.6

Chocolate Muffins

Prep time: 10 minutes| **Cook time:** 10 minutes| **Servings:** 7

Ingredients:

- 3 tablespoons cocoa
- ½ cup Erythritol
- 2 eggs
- 1 teaspoon baking soda
- 1 tablespoon lemon juice
- 1 cup coconut flour
- 1 cup plain yogurt
- ½ teaspoon salt
- 1 teaspoon olive oil

Directions:

Beat the eggs in a mixing bowl. Add the cocoa and mix well. Combine the baking soda with the lemon juice and add to the egg mixture, mixing well. Add Erythritol and yogurt and mix again. Add the salt and coconut flour. Mix well using a hand mixer, until smooth batter forms. Spray the muffin forms with olive oil. Pour the batter into the muffin forms until halfway full. Place the muffins forms in the pressure cooker. Set to "Pressure" mode and close the lid. Cook the muffins for 10 minutes. When the muffins are cooked, remove them from the pressure cooker. Let the muffins rest, then remove them from the muffin forms and serve.

Nutrition: calories 123, fat 4.4, fiber 7.6, carbs 29, protein 6.3

Pineapple Whisked Cake

Prep time: 15 minutes| **Cook time:** 30 minutes| Servings: **10**

Ingredients:

- 9 ounces pineapple, canned
- 4 eggs
- 1 cup almond flour
- 1 cup sour cream
- 1 teaspoon baking soda
- 1 tablespoon lemon juice
- 1 teaspoon cinnamon
- ½ cup erythritol
- 2 tablespoons butter

Directions:

Beat the eggs in the mixing bowl and whisk them with the help of the whisker. After this, add sour cream and continue to whisk the mixture for 1 minute more. Then add baking soda and lemon juice. Stir the mixture gently. Then add Erythritol, cinnamon, butter, and almond flour. Mix the mixture up with the help of the hand mixer for 5 minutes. Then chop the canned pineapples and add them to the dough. Mix up the dough with the help of the spoon. Then pour the dough in the pressure cooker and close the lid. Cook the dish at the manual mode for 30 minutes. When the time is over – open the pressure cooker and check if the cake is cooked. Remove the cake from the pressure cooker and chill it well. Slice the cake and serve. Enjoy!

Nutrition: calories 176, fat 14.2, fiber 1.7, carbs 16.7, protein 5.5

Lime Pie

Prep time: 30 minutes| **Cook time:** 30 minutes| **Servings:** 12

Ingredients:

- 1 teaspoon baking powder
- 1 cup whey
- 1 teaspoon salt
- 1 cup Erythritol
- 1 lime
- 1 teaspoon cinnamon
- 1 tablespoon butter
- 1 teaspoon cardamom
- 2 cups coconut flour

Directions:

Combine the baking powder, whey, and Erythritol in a mixing bowl. Mix well. Add the coconut flour, cardamom, butter, cinnamon, and salt. Mix well and knead the dough. Leave the dough in the bowl under the towel in the warm place for 10 minutes. Slice the limes. Make the layer from the limes in the pressure cooker. Pour the dough in the pressure cooker and flatten it. Close the pressure cooker lid and cook at "Pressure" for 20 minutes. When the pie is cooked, open the pressure cooker lid and let the pie rest. Turn the pie onto a serving plate. Slice the pie and serve.

Nutrition: calories 96, fat 3, fiber 8.3, carbs 31.5, protein 2.9

Sweet Pudding

Prep time: 10 minutes| **Cook time:** 21 minutes| **Servings:** 5

Ingredients:

- 1 cup heavy cream
- ½ cup half and half
- 2 tablespoons starch
- 4 egg yolk
- 2 tablespoons Erythritol
- 1 teaspoon ground cardamom
- 1 teaspoon vanilla extract

Directions:

Whisk the heavy cream, then add the half and half and starch. Whisk the mixture for another minute. Add egg yolks and use a hand mixer to combine the mixture. Add Erythritol, ground cardamom, and vanilla extract. Mix well for another minute. Place the cream mixture in the glass form. Put the trivet in the pressure cooker and add the glass form with the uncooked pudding. Close the pressure cooker lid Cook at "Pressure" for 21 minutes. Remove the pudding from the pressure cooker and chill in the refrigerator for a couple of hours before serving.

Nutrition: calories 175, fat 15.3, fiber 0.1, carbs 11, protein 3.4

Strawberry Cheesecake

Prep time: 10 minutes| **Cook time:** 24 minutes| Servings: **6**

Ingredients:

- 1 cup strawberries
- 1 cup cream
- 2 eggs

- ½ cup Erythritol
- 7 ounces almond arrowroot crackers
- 5 tablespoon butter
- 1 teaspoon vanilla sugar
- ¼ teaspoon nutmeg
- 3 tablespoons low-fat caramel

Directions:

Crush the crackers well and combine them with the butter. Mix well until smooth. Beat the eggs in a mixing bowl. Add the sugar, vanilla Erythritol, nutmeg, and cream. Whisk the mixture well. Wash the strawberries and slice them. Put the cracker mixture in the pressure cooker and flatten it to make the crust. Pour the cream mixture into the crust and flatten it using a spoon. Dip the sliced strawberries in the cream mixture and close the pressure cooker lid. Cook at "Pressure" mode for 24 minutes. When the cooking time ends, remove the cheesecake from the pressure cooker carefully and chill it in the refrigerator. Sprinkle the cheesecake with the caramel, cut into slices and serve.

Nutrition: calories 148, fat 13.4, fiber 0.5, carbs 21.2, protein 2.4

Pumpkin Pudding

Prep time: 10 minutes| **Cook time:** 35 minutes| **Servings:** 7

Ingredients:

- 1 pound pumpkin
- 1 tablespoon pumpkin pie spice
- 3 tablespoons cream
- 1 teaspoon vanilla extract
- 4 cups of water
- 1 teaspoon butter

Directions:

Peel the pumpkin and chop it. Place the pumpkin in the pressure cooker and add water. Close the pressure cooker lid and cook at "Pressure" mode for 20 minutes. Strain the pumpkin and mash it using a fork. Sprinkle the pumpkin with the pumpkin pie spices, vanilla extract, butter, and cream. Mix well until smooth. Pour the pumpkin mixture into a large ramekin, wrap it with aluminum foil, and place it in the pressure cooker trivet. Pour the water in the pressure cooker, avoiding the ramekin. Close the pressure cooker lid and cook at "Sauté" mode for 15 minutes. Remove the pudding from the pressure cooker and let it rest. Remove the foil and serve.

Nutrition: calories 26, fat 1, fiber 0.8, carbs 4, protein 0.6

Cinnamon Apple Cake

Prep time: 10 minutes| **Cook time:** 18 minutes| **Servings:** 10

Ingredients:

- 1 teaspoon cinnamon
- ½ cup Erythritol
- 1 cup coconut flour
- 1 egg
- 1 apple
- 1 cup sour cream
- 1 tablespoon vanilla sugar
- 1 teaspoon ground ginger
- 5 ounces butter
- 1 tablespoon orange juice
- 12 teaspoons lemon zest

Directions:

Beat the egg in the mixing bowl and whisk for a minute. Add the coconut flour, sour cream, vanilla sugar, orange juice, and lemon zest. Mix until smooth. Remove the seeds from the apple and dice. Sprinkle the chopped apple with Erythritol, cinnamon, and ground ginger. Mix well and combine it with the dough, mixing well. Melt the butter and add it to the dough and stir well. Add the apple dough in the pressure cooker. Close the lid and cook at "Pressure" for 18 minutes. When the cooking time ends, open the pressure cooker lid and let the cake rest. Remove the cake from the pressure cooker and transfer it to a serving plate. Slice it and serve.

Nutrition: calories 225, fat 18, fiber 5.6, carbs 23.9, protein 3.2

Hot Vanilla Shake

Prep time: 10 minutes| **Cook time:** 3 minutes| **Servings:** 3

Ingredients:

- 1 cup almond milk
- 2 tablespoons swerve
- 1 teaspoon vanilla extract
- 1 tablespoon almond flour
- 2 tablespoons butter
- 1 tablespoon walnuts, chopped

Directions:

Pour almond milk in the Ninja Foodie. Add swerve and vanilla extract. After this, add butter and close the lid. Cook the liquid on High-pressure mode for 3 minutes. Then allow natural pressure release for 10 minutes. Add almond flour and mix up the liquid until smooth. Add walnuts and stir gently.

Pour the cooked cake in the serving glasses and serve warm.

Nutrition: calories 286, fat 29.4, fiber 2.2, carbs 8.7, protein 3

Strawberry Pie

Prep time: 15 minutes| **Cook time:** 15 minutes| **Servings:** 4

Ingredients:

- 1 cup almond flour
- 1|3 cup butter, softened
- 1 tablespoon swerve
- 1 teaspoon baking powder
- ¼ cup almond milk
- ¼ cup strawberries, sliced

Directions:

Make the batter: mix up together almond flour, softened butter, swerve, baking powder, and almond milk. Whisk it until smooth. Pour the mixture in the Ninja Foodie. Place the sliced strawberries over the batter and press them gently to make the berry layer. Close and seal the lid. Set High-pressure mode and cook pie for 15 minutes. Then allow natural pressure release for 5 minutes. Chill the pie well and cut it into servings.

Nutrition: calories 214, fat 22.5, fiber 1.3, carbs 7.4, protein 2.1

Blondies

Prep time: 15 minutes| **Cook time:** 10 minutes| **Servings:** 6

Ingredients:

- 1 teaspoon baking powder
- 1 teaspoon lemon juice
- 4 tablespoons butter, softened
- 1 cup almond flour
- ¼ cup flax meal
- 3 tablespoons Erythritol
- 1 teaspoon vanilla extract
- 2 tablespoons coconut flakes

Directions:

In the mixing bowl mix up together all the ingredients and knead the smooth and non-sticky dough.

Place the dough in the Ninja Foodie and cut it into small bars. Close the lid and cook on High-pressure mode for 10 minutes. Then allow natural pressure release for 10 minutes more. Chill the cooked dessert well and transfer on the plate.

Nutrition: calories 123, fat 12.3, fiber 2, carbs 3.1, protein 2.2

Pumpkin Cake

Prep time: 15 minutes| **Cook time:** 25 minutes| **Servings:** 10

Ingredients:

- 3 cups canned pumpkin
- 1 teaspoon cinnamon
- 3 cup coconut flour
- 2 eggs
- 1 tablespoon baking powder
- 1 tablespoon apple cider vinegar
- 1|3 cup Erythritol
- 1 teaspoon vanilla extract
- 1 teaspoon olive oil
- ½ cup walnuts
- 1 teaspoon salt

Directions:

Mash the canned pumpkin well. Combine the coconut flour, baking powder, apple cider vinegar, Erythritol, vanilla extract, and salt and stir well. Beat the eggs in the separate bowl. Add the eggs to the coconut flour mixture and stir. Crush the walnuts. Combine the mashed pumpkin and flour mixture together. Knead the dough until smooth. Add crushed walnuts and knead the dough for another minute. Spray the pressure cooker with olive oil. Add the pumpkin dough and flatten it into the shape of the cake. Close the pressure cooker lid. Set at «Pressure" mode and cook the cake for 25 minutes. Check if the cake is cooked using a toothpick, and remove it from the pressure cooker. Let it rest, slice and serve.

Nutrition: calories 228, fat 8.9, fiber 17.1, carbs 31.6, protein 8.2

Lemon Curd

Prep time: 10 minutes| **Cook time:** 13 minutes| **Servings:** 5

Ingredients:

- 4 tablespoons butter
- ½ cup Erythritol
- 3 egg yolks
- 3 tablespoons lemon zest
- 1 cup lemon juice
- 1 teaspoon vanilla extract

Directions:

Place the butter in a blender and add Erythritol. Blend the mixture for 2 minutes. Add the egg yolks and lemon zest. Blend the mixture for 3 minutes. Add the lemon juice and vanilla extract. Blend for 30 seconds. Pour water in the pressure cooker and place the trivet inside. Pour the curd mixture into glass jars and transfer them in the pressure cooker. Close the pressure cooker lid and cook the lemon curd on "Pressure" mode for 13 minutes. When the lemon curd is cooked, release the pressure and remove the glass jars with the lemon curd from the pressure cooker. For the best results, chill the lemon curd in the refrigerator for at least 8 hours.

Nutrition: calories 130, fat 12.3, fiber 0.4, carbs 2.3, protein 2.2

Applesauce

Prep time: 10 minutes| **Cook time:** 16 minutes| **Servings:** 5

Ingredients:

- ½ pound apples
- 2 cup of water
- 1 teaspoon cinnamon
- 1 teaspoon Erythritol

Directions:

Wash the apples and peel them. Chop the apples and place them in the pressure cooker. Add the water and mix well. Close the lid and cook the apples at "Pressure" for 16 minutes. Release the pressure and open the pressure cooker lid. Transfer the cooked apples to a blender and blend well. Add the cinnamon and Erythritol and blend for another minute until smooth. Chill the applesauce in the refrigerator before serving.

Nutrition: calories 13, fat 0.1, fiber 0.8, carbs 3.5, protein 0.1

Keto Donuts

Prep time: 15 minutes| **Cook time:** 6 minutes| **Servings:** 8

Ingredients:

- 1 cup of coconut milk
- 3 eggs, beaten
- 1 teaspoon vanilla extract
- 1cup coconut flour
- ½ cup almond flour
- 1 teaspoon baking powder
- ½ cup Erythritol
- 1 tablespoon ground cinnamon
- 1 teaspoon olive oil

Directions:

Mix up together coconut milk, beaten eggs, vanilla extract, coconut flour, and almond flour. Add baking powder and olive oil. Knead the non-sticky dough. Roll it up and make 8 donuts with the help of the cutter.

Place the donuts in the air fryer basket of Ninja Foodie and close the lid. Cook the donuts at 355F for 3 minutes from each side. After this, mix up together Erythritol and ground cinnamon. Coat every cooked donut in the cinnamon mixture.

Nutrition: calories 204, fat 14.2, fiber 7.9, carbs 26.4, protein 6.3

Chocolate Lava Ramekins

Prep time: 10 minutes| **Cook time:** 10 minutes| **Servings:** 4

Ingredients:

- ½ cup Erythritol
- 3 whole eggs
- 1 cup coconut flour
- 1-ounce chocolate
- 4 egg yolks
- 1 teaspoon vanilla sugar
- 8 ounces butter
- 1 teaspoon instant coffee

Directions:

Beat the whole eggs in a mixing bowl. Add the egg yolks and continue to whisk for a minute. Add the Erythritol and mix well using a hand mixer. Melt the chocolate and butter. Add the melted chocolate to the egg mixture slowly. Add the coconut flour, instant coffee, and vanilla sugar. Mix until smooth. Pour the chocolate mixture into ramekins and place them in the pressure cooker trivet. Transfer the trivet in the pressure cooker. Close the pressure cooker lid and set it to "Bake|Roast." Cook for 10 minutes. When the cooking time ends, open the pressure cooker and remove the trivet. Let the ramekins cool for a few minutes and serve.

Nutrition: calories 644, fat 57.6, fiber 12.1, carbs 23.3, protein 11.6

Grated Pie

Prep time: 25 minutes| **Cook time:** 25 minutes| **Servings:** 7

Ingredients:

- 1 cup strawberries, mashed
- 7 ounces butter
- 1 teaspoon salt
- 1 cup almond flour
- 1 teaspoon vanilla extract
- 1 tablespoon lemon zest
- 1 tablespoon turmeric
- 1 teaspoon nutmeg
- ½ teaspoon ground ginger

Directions:

Grate the butter in a mixing bowl. Sprinkle it with the salt, vanilla extract, lemon zest, turmeric, nutmeg, and ground ginger. Sift the almond flour into the bowl and knead the dough using your hands. Place the dough in the freezer for 15 minutes. Remove the dough from the freezer and cut it in half. Grate the one part of the dough in the pressure cooker. Sprinkle the grated dough with the strawberries. Flatten it well to make a layer. Grate the second part of the dough in the pressure cooker. Close the lid and cook at "Pressure" mode for 25 minutes. When the cooking time ends, transfer the pie to a serving plate and let it rest. Cut into slices and serve.

Nutrition: calories 309, fat 31.3, fiber 2.5, carbs 6.2, protein 3.9

Lemon Flan

Prep time: 15 minutes| **Cook time:** 20 minutes| **Servings:** 4

Ingredients:

- ¼ cup Erythritol
- 3 tablespoons water
- ½ cup coconut cream
- ½ cup cream
- 2 eggs
- ½ teaspoon salt
- 1 tablespoon lemon juice
- 1 teaspoon lemon zest
- 1 teaspoon vanilla extract

Directions:

Combine Erythritol and water together into the pressure cooker and preheat it at «Pressure" mode. Stir the mixture continuously until smooth caramel forms. Pour the caramel into the ramekins. Set the pressure cooker to "Sauté" mode. Pour the cream in the pressure cooker and cook it for 30 seconds. Beat the eggs in a mixing bowl. Add the eggs slowly to the preheated cream, stirring constantly. Add the salt, lemon zest, vanilla extract, and coconut cream. Add the lemon juice and mix well. Cook for 1 minute, stirring constantly. Pour the cream mixture into the ramekins. Place the ramekins in the pressure cooker trivet and transfer it to the pressure cooker. Close the pressure cooker lid. Cook for 8 minutes at "Pressure." Remove the ramekins from the pressure cooker and chill them in the refrigerator for several hours before serving.

Nutrition: calories 181, fat 16.82, fiber 0.5, carbs 3.27, protein 5.12

Ingram Content Group UK Ltd.
Milton Keynes UK
UKHW051107300323
419409UK00008B/421